Cover designed by Robbie Powell

Printed in the United States of America

First Printing: Dec 2018

ISBN-9781790341184

Grateful thanks to all who have journeyed with us. While not everyone is mentioned by name, we so appreciate all you have given. It's been good fun, hasn't it?

Special thanks to a number of friends who helped produce this book - Robbie for designing the front cover, Wendy for proof reading and huge thanks to Philippa for sterling work as editor and all-round encourager.

The portraits on the cover are of the people featured in this book and some of those making up the Leadership Teams at Bonny Downs and Royal Docks Community Church.

LOOKING FOR LYDIA

Encounters that shape the Church

Sally Mann

Sally and Dave love their community. They have a jealous passion to see it thrive. They have resilience which comes from long-term commitment; knowing their dreams of what God might do will take more than a few years of committed service, but decades, and perhaps generations, to achieve. They seek deep transformation in the places they serve – bringing structural changes like good education, just governance, and improving the health and well-being of all their neighbours. Alongside this they have built lively, inclusive, Christian congregations. We should listen to their story.

Steve Chalke
Founder & Leader Oasis Global

In all the window dressing around how to fix the church or make it more connected to our massively disruptive times Looking for Lydia changes the conversation. It turns most of our pretentions on their head as it brings us back to the God who radically meets us in the other. The story in this book is grounded in the practiced life of a community of God's people. I can't recommend it more highly. It's the disruptive Spirit calling us to God's future.

Alan J Roxburgh
Journal of Missional Practice & The Missional Network

FOREWORD BY ASH
BARKER

This book is what the world needs now, from a voice we need to hear. Sally Mann is the fourth of five generations living and ministering in one East End community, with a PhD and five lifetimes of stories. Her experiences will make you laugh, cry and, if you pay attention, help you see how much-needed change can happen.

In our 'fake news' climate with a rapidly rising tide of opinions and arguments, adding more ideas might not make much difference. Example, however, really demonstrates what is possible. Wow! This story can *show* more than *tell* what is needed today. This is the inspiring genius of Sally's book. It should be read by anybody angry and discontented with the status quo.

Sally brilliantly connects Biblical characters with contemporary people and shows how these individuals have helped shape over 150 years of her family's ministry in one East London neighbourhood. I have had the great privilege of meeting some of these five generations and seeing this work-in-progress. It's not always pretty, at times it is heart-breaking, but what God has done through this family is transformative. In this book Sally allows us to hear and see what is etched in the built and natural environment of this place: the funny, the tragic, and the courageous stories that emerge. This can inspire and inform us all.

Sally and Dave are unsung heroes – when in reality they should be sung about loudly as national treasures. They and their little neighbourhood in the East End can easily be overlooked, but we need to pay attention to what God is doing here. As Sally writes: "There is something heroic about staying put in the shifting sands of East London. For us, staying is the new moving (in the inner city at least). Ours is a story of journeying through staying put and most of all, *of looking for Lydia: living out an adventurous faith by engaging with people who expand your ideas about what it means to follow Jesus and build community."* Could this book inspire us to be more courageously planted and see fruit we might miss if we move on too soon?

This particular book is a challenge in many ways, not least because it is so particular! It's about what one particular family in five generations has seen happen in one particular neighbourhood. Yet, this is the genius of this book: it avoids mere generalities and easy steps to success. It focuses in on what happens when we love our particular God and love particular people in a particular place. Could it be that these deep relationships are an antidote to skimming the surface of our shallow world, and missing the real changes that are possible?

Margaret Mead once wrote, "Never doubt that a small group of thoughtful, committed people can change the world: Indeed, it's the only thing that ever has." It would be just like God to use this little, placed community of committed people to change the world. I pray and hope that this book will help do that.

CONTENTS

PROLOGUE

It was once assumed that being a missionary meant making a physical journey. The 'sent out' were the pioneers. Our experience is the opposite. My family have lived in the same four streets in East London for five generations, serving the local community through the same church, Bonny Downs Baptist Church. I hadn't really paid much attention to this until we were contacted by the *Journal of Missional Practice* in Spring 2016. And now we are a story. I have a whole new vocabulary. I am made over. According to current missional parlance I am a 'remainer'. Or I could possibly be a 'New Friar' or an 'Intentional Neighbour'.

My family has become conspicuous by our very lack of movement: we are a missional specimen. I had wondered if my family's enduring call to the East End wasn't best described as a lack of imagination. But I prefer this new narrative. It sounds heroic. And I realise there is something heroic about staying put in the shifting sands of East London. For us, staying is the new moving (in the inner city at least). Ours is a story of journeying through staying put and most of all, *of looking for Lydia: living out an adventurous faith by engaging with people who expand your ideas about what it means to follow Jesus and build community.*

Not only am I the fourth of five generations of a family who have served God in one neighbourhood church, but in my mum's words 'my family live so near I could spit and reach them'. Five households of my immediate family live on one road, with three more on adjoining streets: my parents; parents-in-law; sister; brother; sister-in-law; son and daughter plus spouses and children. And it's not a big street. I know. It's weird. It's especially odd because we have stayed, or moved back into, an area from which our 'white East-Ender tribe' is leaving in droves. There was even a documentary on BBC1 about it in 2016, 'The Last Whites of the East End', all about our borough of Newham. It's not just the white Eastenders who are on the move. to According to the 2011 Census, 21% of the population of East Ham Central were new arrivals in the four years prior (the national average is 3%). The largest growing ethnic group in Newham is from Eastern Europe. Which is why, playing football for his primary school, my son attracted the attention of the woman standing next to me: 'That Lithuanian kid's doing well!' I recognised, at that moment, that not only was Mikey the only white boy in his class but, in Newham, but with his blond hair he would be assumed to be Eastern European.

The pace of change is dizzying. Waves of mass migration, the physical reshaping of gentrification and the push factor of rocketing house prices all mean that I live in the midst of perpetual motion. Newham is among the youngest boroughs nationally and one of the most ethnically diverse globally. Less than 20% of Newham residents are 'White/British'. This is why staying, paradoxically, involves a great deal of journeying. Might those who 'move on' have less experience of change than those who feel called to stay? I have come to believe that many who move from the East End of London, or any inner city, do so to seek the comfort of ethnic conformity through the lens of cultural nostalgia. That's why I can eat a great Somali meal, drink coffee in a Romanian patisserie, buy my bread from an Afghan bakery, but need to go to Essex for pie and mash. What better way to encounter the Other than to stay put and build community in a multi-everything, changing place?

This is the story of 'missional remainers': people who have discerned that following Jesus, for them, means staying put, showing up and being deeply committed to a small geographic place. This *place* holds great sway over how we invest our lives. Of course, remaining in one place for generations won't be how everyone experiences their call to follow Jesus! That said, this story is written partly to challenge the idea that we can dislocate our spiritual lives from the actual places we live, or that we can be disciples without an experience of community. Both of these misconceptions seem to be spreading in the West. They are ideas which do not fit with my reading of Scripture at all, but seem more allied to contemporary principles of individualism. In our call to remain, we seem to have fallen hopelessly in love with a particular, and fairly peculiar, place. We find our sense of who we are in its much bigger story; one which spans generations of our family and perhaps has roots in a much older tale. As we reflect on 20 years of building community churches in the East End of

London, we see our how our story is woven into a more ancient one – the Biblical story of Paul's missionary journeys in the Book of Acts. In our book we invite these stories speak to each other – 're-membering' the Biblical account through our own experiences and imaginations. The Book of Acts is full of surprising encounters which shape the early church. Paul meets people who confirm, challenge and stretch how he sees himself as a disciple of Jesus and as a missionary of the Gospel. This has been our experience too.

As we tell our story we have provided places to pause for thought and hope these will invite you into the story as well.

1. LOOKING FOR LYDIA

My family's story began in the mid-19th century as my great grandparents were sucked into the vortex of urbanisation and industrialisation that led them to London. One branch from Somerset followed the promise of work, another of Jewish migrants fled European persecution, both arriving in an area of present-day East Ham called 'Bonny Downs'. Notorious for its poverty, four roads of slum housing were built for the families of workers at the gas and chemical works in Beckton. They were surrounded by the boggy marshes of the River Roding.[1] The success of Victorian engineering brought the waste from the city of London to Beckton, but the planners were rather less interested in the wellbeing of the workers. The local sewage works stood opposite a hospital for infectious diseases; it took many decades to figure this one out. Men worked at the gas and chemical works, stoking fires which blackened their skin, parched their throats and shortened their lives. At the turn of the century the life expectancy of working men was in their thirties. Women raised their large families on whatever of their husband's wages they could syphon away from the 'Drum and Monkey' pub. It was on these streets, on Bonny Downs Road, that my grandmother was born – the fourth child in a family of 16 children, 13 surviving to adulthood. Her name was Rose Tribley. She went on to marry a neighbour, Alan Pagan, one of 11 children, who, when his mother died, spent years in a workhouse until he was

---

[1] Pictures of the history of Bonny Downs, and of many of scenes and people described in this story are available on the www.bonnydownschurch.org website under the 'Looking for Lydia' tab.

rescued by a sister and came to live on Bonny Downs Road. So, the story of my family's call to stay and serve in this area begins with her, the wonderfully named Rose Pagan.

And it begins with a pioneer missionary, 'Pa' Howe. Sporting the most Victorian of facial adornment, Charles Westerman Howe had somewhat better origins than his soon-to-be parishioners in Bonny Downs. He lived in an adjoining borough, Barking, and against local advice crossed the 'Downs' on his commute to a job in the City. There, as folklore has it, he witnessed 60 impoverished children playing without shoes and a community so God-forsaken that he asked his church, East Ham Baptist, to sponsor him to begin a missional work there. He began by doing what many missionaries do – something entirely irrelevant and doomed to failure: he handed out tracts of Spurgeon's sermons to the illiterate people he had come to rescue. Fortunately for them this was a short-lived venture as Howe realised he would have to start somewhere a little further back in the scheme of salvation.

And this is where Pa Howe's story intersects with a much older one – two thousand years older. It's the story of looking for, and meeting, Lydia. The original Lydia is the first convert on European soil. She was one of many life-changing encounters the apostle Paul would have as he set about spreading his message of Jesus. Both St Paul and Pa Howe needed to meet people who would change their approach to mission, change their understanding of 'church' and even reframe how they understood the Good News of Jesus. If we are willing to search for and find 'Lydia', we can meet those who will do the same for us. It's the 'Lydias' who broaden our understanding of how God might be ahead of us, at work in surprising people, inviting us to join in.

It's time we met Lydia.

Acts 16: 6-15 (NIV)
Next Paul and Silas travelled through the area of
Phrygia and Galatia, because the Holy Spirit had
prevented them from preaching the word in the
province of Asia at that time. 7 Then coming to the
borders of Mysia, they headed north for the

province of Bithynia, but again the Spirit of Jesus did not allow them to go there. ⁸ So instead, they went on through Mysia to the seaport of Troas.

⁹ That night Paul had a vision: A man from Macedonia in northern Greece was standing there, pleading with him, 'Come over to Macedonia and help us!' ¹⁰ So we decided to leave for Macedonia at once, having concluded that God was calling us to preach the Good News there.

¹¹ We boarded a boat at Troas and sailed straight across to the island of Samothrace, and the next day we landed at Neapolis. ¹² From there we reached Philippi, a major city of that district of Macedonia and a Roman colony. And we stayed there several days.

¹³ On the Sabbath we went a little way outside the city to a riverbank, where we thought people would be meeting for prayer, and we sat down to speak with some women who had gathered there.

¹⁴ One of them was Lydia from Thyatira, a merchant of expensive purple cloth, who worshipped God. As she listened to us, the Lord opened her heart, and she accepted what Paul was saying. ¹⁵ She and her household were baptised, and she asked us to be her guests. 'If you agree that I am a true believer in the Lord' she said, 'come and stay at my home.' And she urged us until we agreed.

'Lydia' is never the person you set out to meet, neither is she in the place you expect to find her. But unless you meet her you might as well hand out Spurgeon's sermons to illiterate people. Pa Howe met Rose

Tribley, my grandmother, who at the time was a nit-infested, straggly-haired, bare-footed, skinny girl with an alcoholic father and an incompetent mother. And she was his Lydia. She, among others of her type, changed the way he would do mission. He saw the abuse she lived with and he offered to take her into his home, under the guise of being 'in service' to his wife and a companion for his children. In modern phrasing, his ecclesiology was being shaped by his missiology. He started to meet the community's needs. And it became his life-long work. He hired the backroom of a rag shop on Bonny Downs Road where he taught his newly adopted parishioners to read. Next, he took steps to stop so many dying in the waves of epidemics which would sweep through the area. Pa Howe visited the slums week in week out, changing out of his city suit to nurse his parish through cholera and typhoid epidemics. Every year he organised 'horse-drawn brake outings' to Langdon Hills to get people away from the smog. His little flock became part of the temperance movement, with local women campaigning against the tyranny of alcohol abuse and 'taking the pledge'. In the 1930s he led them to save enough money to erect their own mission building on the corner of Bonny Downs Road (my grandfather Alan Pagan helped put in the windows). He loved and served these people as their pastor for over fifty years. Just before he died, to ensure the continual presence of that church, he affiliated the 'Bonny Downs Mission' to the London Baptist Association. He did all this as a bi-vocational man with no formal training. And my mum says he couldn't preach for toffee. But he knew how to love the hell out of the place he was called to and he knew it would take more than a few years.

Pa Howe was not the first missionary to make an unpromising start, as Acts 16 reveals. This is an intriguing account of Paul trying, and almost failing, to launch his second mission trip. Perhaps the problem is because, after the first trip, he thinks he knows what to do. The geography at the start of the passage hints that Paul begins with a plan to replicate his earlier successful journey and stay within broken ground.

Fixing the Billboard

When I reflect on this, it seems the Church in the West hasn't journeyed far beyond verse seven of Acts 16. The Church's attention seems focussed on fixing itself, tracking back over familiar ground, doing things it has always done, replicating early missional journeys, frustrated that they aren't working. The Church produces hundreds of 'how to' books promising programmes to guarantee church growth; ten steps to copy; prototypes to download; the endless round of seminars promising there is a definite fix, a magic way to force God to 'grow this church, now!' In the main we have focused on 'attractional church models' with a little bit of safe foray in to the community; perhaps a Toddler Group? Often this is done so that congregations can invite people to Sunday worship services and, if we are frank, nab families from other congregations with our better youth ministry, funkier bands and fresher coffee. But it is not working.

By attempting to fix the marketing and style of Sunday worship services, Evangelical Christianity seems focussed on patching up the 'billboard' of our churches.[2] By this I mean, we tend to think about fixing our structures and rebranding our institutions, rather than considering the possibility that there is a broader vision of God's activity in the world beyond what we have known and what we have seen. Billboards are man-made structures which both show and obscure images. The picture on the billboard is manufactured, the view behind it is wilder, wider and of an altogether different magnitude. In a simple sense, billboards are marketing tools, inviting interest and promoting a good or service. Churches might see themselves as 'billboards' for the broader reality of following Jesus, of being part of the Kingdom of God. Sometimes they do this well, operating as signs of a different way of life; a different way to be community. There's much to celebrate about church life. Being part of a local church has enriched my life with love, laughter, challenge and wisdom. But sometimes our church structures can become dilapidated, no longer fit-for-purpose. More worryingly, sometimes the messages churches present can over simplify divine mystery and promote a rigid, parcelled up, two-dimensional 'Gospel'. Then churches can act like billboards obscuring the broader view of God's untamed, beautiful Kingdom. When we focus all our attention on fixing the Church, much of what we call 'mission' becomes a counterfeit attempt to build congregations or reinforce a worldview rather than reach the unreached and love the unloved. So much 'fixing the billboard'.

As I read Acts 16 I am forced to ask, 'What if it's God who is shaking this 'billboard' apart?' It's not unthinkable that while the Church is trying to fix itself, it's God who is shaking it. In Acts it's the Holy Spirit preventing Paul

---

[2] This metaphor came out of reflecting in Acts 16 with the Editorial Board of the *Journal of Missional Practice*. A discussion about it is on their website http://journalofmissionalpractice.com/beyond-the-billboard-1-talk/

preaching the word. It's the Spirit of Jesus forming a roadblock. God has other things in mind than re-treading old ground. Which begs the question, 'What is *beyond the billboard* and how can we go there?' I have started to seek an answer to this by asking, what does the Christian community look like when the church is not just at the heart of the community, but the community is truly at the heart of the church?

Dance of Agency

One thing I notice as I read Acts 16 is the 'dance of agency.' The words describing God's actions have clarity and intention: 'forbidding'; 'not allowing'; speaking in visions. The experience of the missionaries is decidedly messier! They 'attempt' journeys, are 'convinced', 'suppose' and are 'prevailed upon'. God and people are at work, but God is always the prime mover. In Acts 16, Paul's team journey to a place where the Sprit is already at work, and they are invited to join in. Lydia is a 'worshipper' before they arrive. Mission is fundamentally a *misseo dei*; it's what God does because of who God is. To join in requires an open spirituality, sense of exploration, discernment and obedience. In this way missional projects are provisional and adventuresome exercises, seeking to discover what God is already up to. They lead into unexpected territories and surprising encounters. There will be false starts. Maybe Paul's early attempts to start his second missionary journey were necessary stepping stones? The geography of Acts 16 is revealing, so many islands and ports on the way to the new European mainland. Perhaps Paul's team could be directed precisely because they were already moving? Anyone who has steered a bike knows that active motion is essential. The church, the *ecclesia*, is a 'sent out' community, first and foremost.[3] It is impossible to steer a monument, less of a challenge to direct a movement.

Encountering 'the Other'

There's another gem here. As they journey, Paul's team increasingly encounter God through unexpected 'strangers'; they experience *alterity*. This is the experience of being challenged and changed by meeting the 'other', the person you were perhaps taught to fear, to look down on, or even hate. This was a great theme of Jesus' ministry. Many of his parables

---

[3] See Mark Lau Branson's 'Ecclesiology and Leadership for the Missional Church' Chapter 4 of Craig 2007 *The Missional Church in Context: Helping Congregations Develop Contextual Ministry. Grand Rids, Mich.*

play on the idea of encountering Samaritans; it's their faith and honourable lifestyle which provides the twist in the tale. Jesus takes Samaritan people seriously and goes out of his way to meet them. The woman at the Well is a great example (John 4:4-42). The disciples fuss about food and cultural norms. Jesus has a great theological debate and changes the outsider into a missionary. The experience of alterity is deeper than challenging prejudice. It's about how you see yourself, and potentially, God. Globalisation, mass migration and the growth of a 'precariat'[4] class of the persistently poor, have increased opportunities for Westerners to meet the 'other', the stranger, the outcast right on their doorstep. Cultural representation teaches us the 'others' are the dangerous outsiders in our midst. In the face of so much difference, one option is to shore up a sense of identity by exclusionary practices, splitting into 'Them and Us' camps. Christians are no less prone to this. But there is an alternative. Many theologians are considering what God might be doing in inviting the West into so many opportunities to encounter 'the other' among our neighbours; to meet 'Lydia'. A 'theology of embrace' is emerging. Could meeting the 'stranger' invite us to open up our sense of who we are, to shift from excluding the stranger to embracing them, and finding as we make space for them, that a new space opens up within us? As we encounter and embrace the very people we have been told to exclude our own sense of who we are opens up.[5] How marvellous! Staying put in Newham is a shortcut to precisely this experience! Mass migration, the dissolution of mono-cultures, the diversity of my particular multi-everything borough provide wonderful opportunities for just such engagements, for alterity to change how we see others, ourselves and God.

How ironic that Lydia originated in Asia, Thyatira, where Paul was 'forbidden by the Holy Spirit' to go at the start of this passage! Paul ventures into Europe and the first person to come to faith is an immigrant Asian woman. This is not what Paul expected. God gives a vision of a *Macedonian man* pleading for help (Acts 16:5) but it is a *migrant woman* who is the key to the Church reaching Europe (maybe God knew Paul mightn't have gone otherwise?) Her 'imploring' them to stay unlocks the church plant at Philippi. And so, the Gospel stumbles into Europe through

---

4 Guy Standing (2011) *The Precariat: A New Dangerous Class*, Bloomsbury Press.
5 See Volf *Exclusion and Embrace: A theological Exploration of Identity, Otherness, and Reconciliation (Nashville, TN: Abingdon Press, 1996)*

thwarted attempts and risky journeys, visions and decisions, God's agency and human obedience, and through encounters with the 'other'.

Looking for Lydia in East London

This will be the story of our journey in the same physical place, the exact same church, as my grandmother Rose Pagan found real salvation. It is the church I serve as Senior Minister with my husband Dave. It's the story of 20 years of East London ministry as our church left its building and moved into the community in ways which still surprise us. It's the story of growing a church through community organising, setting up a local charity and shoring up the potential for transformative presence in Bonny Downs. And it's the story of church planting in a neighbouring community in the London Dockland. It's the story of jumping fences to cut forgotten playing fields, planting gardens in wastelands, giving a dog communion at a park bench, trespassing to hold baptism services, and of a Muslim Angel Gabriel. It's the story of Dave being barred from entering the community centre he is employed to run, of house sharing, of preparing sermons in a foodbank. It's the story of an adventure to 'look for Lydia' and see more of what the Church looks like beyond the 'billboard' of its institutions. It can never be a 'here's how you can do it' book. But as you read, I hope it gives you a sense of the thrills and spills and I hope it may even cheer on those on similar journeys.

As I reflect, I am struck with the similarities between our story and the people Paul needed to meet to understand mission in the West. We met our Ananias, the person who believes in you. We met many Corneliuses, the people who break down your prejudices. We met Agabus, the truth teller, and we had to stand up to people like Felix, Festus and Agrippa. We thank God for the Priscillas and Aquilas of our story who taught us bi-vocational ministry and shared living. And our story is of course, not only just *our* story. It's the story of the people of God here at Bonny Downs, worshipping in three congregations, and continuing to serve through community projects which now employ over 100 people each year. They are recognisably 'Roman Brothers and Sisters', communities of welcome and refuge. And none of it would have been possible unless we too set out to look for Lydia.

Some questions to reflect on...

*How have **places** shaped your experience of God?*

*Is there a sense of '**call**' involved in where you live now, or is something else dictating this decision?*

*Have you met a '**Lydia**'? - someone who changed the way you now understand what it means to follow Jesus?*

*[For those who feel called to be leaders] How much of your experience of Christian service has been taken up by '**fixing the church**?' How has this left you feeling? Do you have space in your week to meet 'Lydias' – people outside of your usual circle?*

2. MEETING ANANIAS

the person who believes in you

*Acts 9:17 So Ananias went and found Saul. He laid
his hands on him and said, 'Brother Saul, the Lord
Jesus, who appeared to you on the road, has sent
me so that you might regain your sight and be
filled with the Holy Spirit.'*

I t took a large dose of faith to believe that Saul was called by God for a role in the Church. Hadn't he held the coats of the mob who stoned Stephen to death? Wasn't he officially sanctioned to round up Christians? Didn't he represent the exact type of religious zealot that wanted the Jesus sect under their boot? And now he expects to be led by the hand into the heart of the Christian community? That wasn't going to happen. For a start, all other church leaders were first generation eye-witnesses. Their pedigree was proximity to the man Jesus himself. Saul hadn't even met him. And he turns up with some half-baked story of a Damascus-road encounter, feigning blindness. But Ananias knew it was not *Saul* asking to be acknowledged in his calling. It was *God's* instruction. It was precise. Ananias was to be the man to open the door for Saul.

We don't know much about Ananias, but we do know that on the strength of the Spirit's leading, he called Saul 'brother'. Had he not, Saul would have been left in Damascus, blinded by revelation but without an audience to explain it to. What would first-century mission have looked like in the absence of this unlikely leadership candidate? What might the

New Testament have been without the Gospel's greatest apologist? Ananias was the one who stuck his neck out and in obedience to God, said, 'Saul, I believe in you.'

We all need someone who believes in us. This is especially true when we feel called to do something less practiced; something that may involve false starts and high stakes.

For Dave and me it took a while to meet our Ananias, the people who would encourage us and our style of ministry. Neither of us started with a Bible college education or formal training. Today, Dave and I are accredited ministers in the Baptist Union of Great Britain but we are both unlikely candidates.

Beginning Ministry

Dave had about twenty jobs in the years leading up to a call to ministry: training as a journalist; travelling in South America; working in print sales; even test-driving automated trains on the Docklands Light Railway. He joined Bonny Downs Baptist Church when he had to move from the more centrally located area of Bow, and wanted to live within walking distance of West Ham United football ground. East Ham was a cheaper area than Bow and there was a small, community-focussed church around the corner with around 25 adult members and a stunning 17-year-old guitar-playing worship leader (I am writing this story so I can tell it how I like). My training was just as unlikely. From a precocious passion to be an evangelist and change the world, perhaps working in a developing country as a socio-economist, instead, I married Dave at 18. We bought a house directly opposite the original church building on the former Bonny Downs Road, and had three children before I was 25. Church growth through natural reproduction was working well, but left me feeling I had lost my spark. So with family support I started a degree in Theology at a local university, taking extra courses in Philosophy. I took to study like a fish to water, or like a young mother who was suddenly allowed to read, think and write. A first-class Bachelor's degree and winning a bursary for postgraduate study led to a doctorate in Philosophy. I wrote conceptual papers on the Philosophy of Language and a thesis on post-structuralism while paying my way by teaching excluded pupils and tutoring young parents at the local further education college.

Dave was commissioned to be the pastor of Bonny Downs Baptist Church in November 1996. As Baptists, all it took was the discernment of the congregation's members, a vote that confirmed that Dave already *was* operating as their minister, and so, officially, he was. Ironically, this happened at the one time Dave had started a job that was both interesting and offered career potential; his first 'round-peg-round-hole' job, as public relations manager for a local housing association. The decision to go part-time and commit to leading the local church was confirmed in that first year when 12 people were baptised as new Christians. The congregation swelled – to just over 35 members! Within a year the call to lead the church beyond its walls was stirring within Dave. The small 1930s asbestos hut of the church building was creaking at the seams as its small congregation's commitment to engage with the community grew. I love that building, the original 1930s Bonny Downs Mission. I have been baptised, married, and had my children dedicated there, but by the 1990s it was no longer fit for purpose. It housed a coffee morning bringing elders together, was trashed by the weekly open youth group we ran, and worn out by the toddler groups and parties it hosted. And just around the corner, at the other end of the original Bonny Downs Road, was an under-used, council-owned facility in a much newer, bigger building: the 'Wellstead Road Community Centre'. It was mainly a subsidised bar and not the most welcoming place to anyone except the few local families who ran its programme of bingo and cheap beer. It was rumoured that drugs were dealt from the toilets. (This later proved to be true, when one former dealer later joined the church and was given the job of repainting them as an act of penance).

The Well

Dave joined as a member of the Wellstead Road Club. For us, this was the beginning of an excursion into new territory. Much like the beginning of Paul's journey in Acts 16, it was a time of trying new things, beginning to see things differently, and wondering what it was like 'beyond the billboard' of doing things as they had always been done. Bonny Downs Church had always loved its neighbourhood. It remained faithful to the DNA Pastor Howe had written into the church at its inception: meeting needs, showing practical compassion, preaching a simple Gospel of love and grace. But it had always operated from its own building and ran activities 'for' people.[6] This was all to change. An adventure outside of

---

[6] Sam Wells (2018) considers doing thing 'with' rather than 'for' or 'to' people

what we had known as a faith community was about to begin. It started when Dave walked into the Wellstead Road Community Centre. He got a frosty reception. It was clear that the venue was hobbling along; utility suppliers were withdrawing services through lack of payment. When the brewery pulled out and the beer pumps dried up, the existing members put down their pints, walked out and locked the doors behind them. It was 1997. Dave had been in his part-time church role for a matter of months, with a small congregation and very limited finances. But he discerned that an opportunity was opening up for the church to act as 'rebuilders of the city', the vision of God's people in Isaiah 58:12, and so he started negotiations with the council to take on the building's lease. The journey 'beyond the billboard' had begun.

The Book of Acts takes just a few thousand words to cover a 30-year history. Here are the headlines of our early ministry at Bonny Downs. Dave's initial bid to resurrect the community centre was met with suspicion by the local council. Why would they agree to a church controlling one of their facilities? There was some trepidation among the small congregation too. It was decided to form a separate charity, Bonny Downs Community Association (BDCA) to manage the community centre. This placated the council and some of the more hesitant church members, and proved to be a great opportunity to partner with like-minded people outside the church – the barriers between secular and sacred were blurring. Instead of doing good things *to* and *for* its community, Bonny Downs was venturing into the model of doing good things *with* local people. We were starting to discern something beyond the way we had always done things. It was the pattern of a Kingdom ministry; one where mission would shape the life of the church, working *with* our community in partnerships for the common good of the neighbourhood. But there were significant challenges right from the start.

Although it was only twenty years old, the community centre was in terrible repair. The church took a brave decision to invest its total savings and asked members for a sacrificial offering. This provided a £30,000 budget to begin renovations. Saturday work parties were formed to knock out the bar and build a café area in the heart of the centre. Stripping the walls, repairing the floor, clearing out rubbish, these were our 'missional practices' at Bonny Downs. When money ran out to pay for skips, church members volunteered their own cars, filling them with building detritus

by *Incarnational Mission: being with the world*, Canterbury Press.

and offloading them for free at the council depot. It was slow progress, and it became abundantly clear that we had bitten off far more than we could chew. We started to apply for funding, initially asking for a £50,000 grant from a national charity. They looked at us and our project and offered five grand if we could raise the rest of the cash. Dave said at the time that those three years of pushing forward without much evidence of progress were God's grace. When it looked like the project would fail, Dave clung to the truth that whether or not the community centre opened it had been a blessing to bring the church out of its comfort zone. Just when it looked doomed, God started to open doors. Just as in the Acts 16 story of Paul's missional journey, God's agency was so much clearer than our messy forays in the unknown. By coincidence, Dave was at a council meeting where he heard there was an underspend in the borough's housing budget. Although our project didn't strictly meet the criteria, Dave put in a bid to use some of this for the more urgent refurbishment works at the community centre, now renamed 'The Well'. Over a period of weeks, the amount in consideration escalated from £30,000 to £300,000. The council would pay for almost all of the works. The Well would open!

The opening celebration event took place in June 2001. Community projects and ministries which had been run at the old Bonny Downs Church moved in, with a volunteer workforce from the church. Partnerships rapidly formed with like-minded community groups who loved to see the life bubbling in The Well. The first paid BDCA workers were two part-time centre managers; one from the congregation and another local man with experience of managing public buildings. Today The Well is a thriving community hub with an estimated 3,000 visits a week. In 2018, BDCA employed more than 100 people in the course of a year, including sessional staff, the vast majority of whom are from the immediate area. They run an amazing range of projects to reflect BDCA's values of 'Inclusion, Celebration and Empowerment'.[7]

Once the journey out of institutional conformity began, it gathered pace. Dave's social-entrepreneurial spirit was released to tackle other projects. He sought to materialise the vision of Zechariah 8:4-6, of a city living well where old and young are safe and life is abundant.

---

[7] Bonny Downs Community Association website is www.bonnydowns.org

Flanders Field

Even before The Well was open, a holy discontent stirred again in Dave's heart. Just on the other side of the road to the old church building was a nine-acre playing field, gone to seed. Flanders Field was the original ground Pastor Howe had crossed to visit Bonny Downs. In its glory days it was a much-loved school playing field. Bobby Moore, the legendary West Ham and former England football player, was scouted there as a child. But these days were long gone. With waist-high grass, the remnants of a burnt-down wooden pavilion and piles of rubbish, the unkempt field was the scourge of the houses surrounding it. It was a cut-through for burglars and a picture of neglect. Meanwhile, several men from the church shared Dave's passion for football and met in the local park to play odd games. Pete Laing (who would later become CEO of BDCA) and a group of local footballers managed to get keys to the disused field, hired hand-held grass strimmers and started to cut one pitch. Neighbours appreciated the renewed interest in what had become a local eyesore. Dave posted handmade leaflets inviting everyone living around the field to a meeting in the old church hall. Approaching the council again, signs of progress were clear. A local store offered two sit-on mowers for the price of one, which was a good job because one was stolen within days of being delivered.

Today there is a nine-acre fully functioning sports ground on Flanders Field with a £1.2 million pavilion, thanks to funds raised by grant applications from BDCA. [8] It is named after the late Bobby Moore, with his wife's permission. Stephanie Moore officially opened the pavilion in the summer of 2009. Today, alongside the football pitches, it has two grass cricket squares which Dave trained to help maintain. It's the home ground of Newham Cricket Club, and many other football teams and schools use it every day.

We also see physical transformation, a literal reclaiming of wastelands, in the community garden and food growing project called Grow Together, Be Together cultivated in one corner of Flanders Field. We grow food for The Well café and for our neighbours, bringing people together to nurture the land and learn from each other. The community garden hosts four inter-faith celebrations a year. We celebrate Easter and Christmas there, in the heart of our community, and we join our neighbours as they celebrate

---

[8] See Before/After photos of Flanders Field under the 'Looking for Lydia' tab on www.bonnydownschurch.org.

Muslim and Hindu festivals. As we do, we see common ground in which we can truly rejoice, and we see bridges built between faith communities, such as with our local Imam, Sanaullah Sethi.

The pavilion also hosts the NewDay 'Purpose and Belonging' day centre giving people who are homeless or vulnerably housed access to showers and free facilities to wash clothes. This project is managed by BDCA in partnership with a small local charity, Skills Enterprise. This daytime provision grew out of the winter night-shelter, NewWay[9], and found a great home in the pavilion. The venue breaks down the stigma of needing somewhere to wash; everybody showers in a sports pavilion! Adding laundry facilities meant the pavilion could serve another much-needed purpose.

The pavilion also hosts our after-school and holiday clubs, providing great activities for children, leadership training for young leaders and a vital service for working parents. We have learned the value of integrating people with different needs and gifts in one location. Our community is working hard to break down the 'Us and Them' mentality. This means we are always meeting Lydias, the people who challenge us to rethink our mission and blur the boundaries of our faith community.

And, to Dave's greatest joy, Flanders Field is home to West Ham United Over 50s Walking Football Team, which he coaches, playing in the official strip and boasting a number 6 shirt – the number Bobby Moore played in for West Ham. Football, and more specifically West Ham United, is an enduring passion in Dave's life. He jokes that the feeling of running onto a Flanders Field pitch in his Bobby Moore shirt is right there in the Bible: Luke 2:29-30, 'Now let your servant depart in peace...I have seen your salvation!'

The lesson I almost don't wish to recount is this.... sometimes in ministry, don't listen to your wife. When Dave began to strike out and rescue Flanders Field, The Well was still not open, staffing was precarious, and the works were beset by problems. I advised him to let go of the field. I'm more of a ducks-in-a-row person, whereas Dave is a jump-in-the-pond-and-worry-where-the-ducks-land-afterwards person. But, sometimes there's a wave of momentum in community development which means the risk of faith is timely. Dave was right not to listen to my fears. We were already well out of our depth in reinstating a community centre; would it really be such a leap to include a playing field?

---

9 NewWay Project https://www.newwayproject.org/

Learning to be a 'parish'

The lesson we learned from these years is that moving out of the church building, physically and metaphorically, created unexpected momentum. Seeking to restore what was lost and wasted in our neighbourhood reminded the church of its roots, its responsibility to steward every aspect of the neighbourhood. This is a return to the former idea of the Church having a 'parish' with responsibility for more than the spiritual wellbeing of parishioners, but with a duty to maintain healthy, just social and economic structures.[10] It's a vision many are exploring how to live out today. It has fostered movements like the Parish Collective in the USA and the New Parish Conference in the UK[11]. The Journal of Missional Practice gathers grassroots stories from North America and the UK. These stories from local faith communities are usually unnoticed, but deserve to be celebrated and reflected upon to discern the ways that God is at work. [12]

The move to The Well, and all that followed, put our church at the centre of the community, not by asserting power and drawing dividing lines between 'us' and 'them', but by practicing redemptive love and partnering with the community to restore the common good. We have been living Miroslav Volf's 'theology of embrace'[13] before we had the language to explain it; not just as individuals, but as a faith community. By opening ourselves up to 'others', whether in partnering the local council, working alongside the community, and especially in welcoming people who were ignored or feared, we find that we change.

Friends and Family

The late 1990s and early 2000s were adventurous times at Bonny Downs. They were years of 'being church' rather than 'going to church'. We shared these years with a group of friends, Di and Greg Nash, Barbara and Simon Church and Sarah and Pete Laing, among others, as we raised our young families and witnessed the amazing transformations in our area, and ourselves. During these years, Dave's extended family, his parents, sister and brother-in-law, moved into East Ham as 'relocators', drawn by

---

[10] Andrew Rumsey (2017) *Parish: an Anglican theology of place*, SCM Press
[11] See the Parish Collective website https://parishcollective.org/ and, for the UK gathering, http://www.newparishconference.co.uk/
[12] *Journal of Missional Practice* http://journalofmissionalpractice.com/
[13] Volf *Exclusion and Embrace: A theological Exploration of Identity, Otherness, and Reconciliation* (Nashville, TN: Abingdon Press, 1996)

the sense of community at Bonny Downs. Dave's parents' estate agent was completely bemused by their decision to sell their house in Woodford Green and move to Darwell Close, directly opposite the old church mission building. They too committed to the church and BDCA, serving as trustees and helping put financial systems in place. Matthew, our brother-in-law, came up with the new name for the old Wellstead Road Community Centre, and Ros, Dave's sister, designed The Well's first logo. Matthew is the longest serving trustee at BDCA. Over 20 years later, they all still live here. 'Relocators' and 'returners' are perhaps the most pioneering of missional workers. They buck the trend of upward mobility, intentionally moving into areas others might be keen to move out of!

During these early years, time and again, God faithfully blessed our efforts and poured love and healing into the land, the church, the community and us.

Ananias people

So where was our Ananias? Where were the people who believed in our little group as we were starting and struggling to do something entirely new? In all honesty, and somewhat sadly, they have not come from within our denomination. We have not sought, or had, any profile among Baptist colleagues and perhaps have not communicated our journey well to them. When I was ordained in 2014, not one Baptist minister from Newham came to the service. Whenever we have needed to connect with denominational structures we have felt like fish out of water. We don't have the right background, we haven't been through the proper training, we don't measure success by the size of congregations, we don't go to their training events; they just don't scratch where our ministry itches. At the beginning, several people within our own congregation could not fully get behind our efforts to blur the edges of church life into the community, or our focus on community organising as a key part of ministry. One exception was an American couple, Richard and Lia Katz who, unlike us, had lived internationally in 15 different time zones. They gave us time, challenge and encouragement to become better ministers. However, the most vocal Ananias voices came from the wider community. As local people saw the efforts we were making, they voiced their support and approval, and many asked searching, spiritual questions about our motivation.

Decades before we began to lead the missional community at Bonny Downs, Lesslie Newbiggin asked, 'Can the West be converted?' Part of the answer, for Newbiggin was for the local church to be an embassy for the Kingdom of God, to be a place where justice and mercy are enfleshed:

> 'What is true in the position of the social activists is that a Church which exists only for itself and its own enlargement is a witness against the gospel, that the Church exists not for itself and not for its members but as a sign and agent and foretaste of the kingdom of God, and that it is impossible to give faithful witness to the gospel while being indifferent to the situation of the hungry, the sick, the victims of human inhumanity.'[14]

We strongly agree.

Happily, we have met more Christian Ananiases later in the day. As the West revisits a theology of place, the 'remainers' and community developers like us have suddenly received something other than suspicion from institutional church structures and are connecting together in networks of support and encouragement. Staying put, digging in, measuring church impact by community transformation, experiencing discipleship as redemptive local action and reflective praxis, are more in vogue. Renewed interest in Benedictine spirituality has thrown a more positive light on the 'remainers'. Even those who brought into what the missiologist Al Roxburgh describes as the Modernist Wager – 'the more mobile ('free') I am, the better my personal choices and the more fulfilled I become' – have come to question this illusion. A generation of post-modernists attempt to commodify community, to buy into a 'tribe' through consuming the right things or having a shared set of experiences: the gap year; adventure holidays; the round of high adrenalin sports; addiction to reality TV. These may provide some sense of connection in the 'multi-everything' West, but most are the preserve of the privileged, and they are often found to be superficial. Consumeristic attempts at community may meet our need to belong, but exacerbate what they cannot fill: the need to be seen, to be known. In the midst of our culture of materialism, individualism and consumerism, many seek an authentic experience of belonging somewhere.[15] For many, as for us, this has involved a deep

---

[14] Lesslie Newbiggin (1989) *The Gospel in a Pluralist Society*, Eerdmans

[15] Al Roxburgh considers theologies of place from the experience of curating stories of people living as a faithful presence in diverse communities in Issue 10 of

commitment to live in one place and to be immersed in one community. Can the Christian life really be lived without a real commitment to a certain 'place'? Is the remainers 'gift of stability' shining more brightly against a culture of using neighbourhoods as capital investment, and the unquenchable, illusionary promise of upward mobility? Are we looking away from the pick-and-mix, serve-yourself, commodified church that has been popular in the Evangelical movement to the 'slow church' where time is given to work things through in one place at a deeper, costlier level of commitment?

Alongside emerging theologies of place have come the related reconsideration of 'land'. Brueggeman[16] challenges a capitalist, consumerist generation to rethink how we view land. Biblically, land is not given to meet people's needs, but people are given to God's land to care for it. Place matters. Neighbourhoods matter. Disused community buildings and overgrown playing fields matter. The absence of meeting places for true encounters between cultures is not only dangerous, it is sinful.

After nearly 20 years we have found Ananias voices in other Christian leaders, but interestingly, for the most part, they have come with foreign accents. Ash and Anji Barker are our Ananias heroes. After twelve years living and working in Klong Thoey, the largest slum in Thailand, the Barkers relocated to live out immersive community in Winson Green, Birmingham. Meeting them a number of years ago put our small-scale incursions into incarnate ministry into perspective! And they were interested in us. They have visited many times, bringing teams from their community to walk the Bonny Downs streets, visit its centres and fields and squeeze through my mum's back fence to hear her stories.[17] We have taken groups to visit them and their crazy alpacas. Only the Barkers would arrive in Winson Green, Birmingham, and decide to buy a petting zoo for their back garden so that local people can wander in and help look after animals. Ash has invested greatly in us, training seven of our young leaders on the 'Urban Changemakers' project in 2017/18. They are true Ananiases,

the *Journal of Missional Practice* http://journalofmissionalpractice.com/questions-of-place/

[16] Walter Brueggemann (1997) *The Land: Place as Gift, Promise, and Challenge in Biblical Faith.* Fortress Press, 1977,

[17] With Ash's permission there is a picture of this momentous moment on the 'Looking for Lydia' tab at www.bonnydownschurch.org

encouraging, applauding and listening to our story, and then, as the original disciple did, introducing us to a world of other community-developing ministers and missiologists.

Before we knew we had a story worth telling, Ash Barker connected us to Martin Robinson at the *Journal of Missional Practice* who took the time to interview me and Angie Allgood (my sister in ministry in every sense) and tell the story of Bonny Downs. They wrote an article about us and invited my response and reflection. They even invited me to join an international think tank with Mark Lau Branson, Harvey Kwiyani, Mary Publicover, Martin Robinson, Alan Roxburgh, Sara Jane Walker, Fiona Watts and Paul Weston. Suddenly, although I felt like a tiny fish, I was in the right water! Our discussions, sometimes published as webcasts, started to give me the language to frame our experiences of mission and ministry and provided the oxygen to refine this reflection. It was during these think tanks in Toronto, Birmingham and Vancouver that we 'dwelt in the Word' of Acts 16. This is a simple practice of listening to one passage of the Bible, read by different voices, over a number of days or even months. After every reading there is time for quiet reflection before listening to each other's insights. You share what you hear others say and practice deep listening of God's voice through this. These think tank reflections inspired a teaching series in our home congregations, 'Encounters: The People You Need to Meet' which have, in turn, framed this telling of our story. I am blessed to be reimagining church with these folk and with other American friends from the 'Parish Collective' (I also took *them* to my mum's for tea, but I learnt my lesson and took them through the front door).

Ananias listened to Paul's story. He got over the oddness of the man and saw the potential and call God had on his life. He was the gate-keeper to Paul's acceptance in the Jerusalem church. Missional pioneers need an Ananias. And we have found ours. We have even finally felt embraced by the Baptists! My process of accreditation required me to find a local minister to mentor me. I approached Jane Thorington Hassell, a Baptist minister who has served one local church in East London for 30 years and is also married to a Baptist minister. Jane has given me a safe place to grow and struggle over the four years of my probation. Her wisdom has given my confidence to be myself. Dave has found a similar mentor in Steve Chalke. Steve was instrumental in helping us set up Oasis Academy Silvertown, a later part of this story. In Steve, Dave has found someone who is truly committed and marvelously experienced in building inclusive, Christ-centred communities beyond the walls of the church.

We thank the people who have believed in us. As we move to focus on legacy and growing other indigenous leaders, we want to learn how to be an Ananias to others. We all need someone to believe in us. We can be that person for others.

Some questions to reflect on...
*Looking back, who has been your '**Ananias**'?*
How have you been shaped by someone who believes in you? Or, if you have lacked this, have you connected with people who are on a similar journey for mutual encouragement? Is this something you need to give greater attention to?
*[For Leaders] How have you **opened doors** for others?*

3. LISTENING TO AGABUS

– the person who tells you the difficult truth about what is ahead

Acts 21:10-12 After we had been there a number of days, a prophet named Agabus came down from Judea. Coming over to us, he took Paul's belt, tied his own hands and feet with it and said, 'The Holy Spirit says, "In this way the Jewish leaders in Jerusalem will bind the owner of this belt and will hand him over to the Gentiles"'.

Fast forward to 2003. The Well Community Centre and Flanders Field were up and running with a measure of success we could not have imagined. The worshipping congregation at Bonny Downs had quadrupled. Bonny Downs Baptist Church had moved its Sunday worship service into The Well as soon as it opened in 2001. It was a more than a physical move; it was a prophetic stance. Our community was at the heart of our church and we worshipped where the community gathered. We intentionally made 'blurry edges' (a term which stuck to describe our approach) between the worshipping congregation and the wider community using the centre. Within three years our worship services had outgrown the large hall at the Well. In 2005 we were joined by an assistant minister for Bonny Downs and a full-time worker from London City Mission. As space got tight we began meeting in two morning services and experimented with planting a congregation in the pavilion. Our Portuguese speaking home group had also grown, and we encouraged them and their indigenous leaders to plant out as a sister congregation, meeting in the old Bonny Downs building.

'Wild West Silvertown'

It was then that a church-planting Baptist minister, Penny Marsh, saw what BDCA had accomplished and asked Dave to be a trustee of a much smaller project in West Silvertown, in a new urban development called Britannia Village. Penny had been commissioned by the London Baptist Mission Association to plant a church in this new community. Her role was funded by the Baptist Home Mission Fund. Under her leadership, Royal Docks Community Church had been inaugurated. Dave got involved in sharing some of the lessons from BDCA and became a trustee of Penny's project.

Britannia Village is only 4km south of East Ham and part of the same London Borough of Newham, but in many ways it is a different world. East Ham has been an ethnically diverse neighbourhood for many decades. It has a large number of elderly residents as well as young families. But although its population is diverse in terms of ethnicity and age, socio-economically it is very similar: mostly working class. There are very few professional families in East Ham - although this is changing today as gentrification spreads rapidly in Newham. West Silvertown is different. Alongside ethnic diversity it has a striking socio-economic divide. It has some of the poorest and wealthiest Newham residents in one small area. Geographically, Britannia Village is virtually an island community, at the southernmost edge of Newham. The Royal Victoria Dock runs to the north, the River Thames to the south and the River Lea to the east.[18] The area had working docks until 1980. Regeneration began in 1994, pulling down the imposing 1960s tower blocks to build an 'urban village' attracting a new community with a wealthier demographic. Much of the marketing of

---

[18] Pictures and maps of the Royal Docks area on the tab 'Looking for Lydia' at www.bonnydownschurch.org.

Britannia Village was aimed at commuters from Canary Wharf, an extension of the City of London and a hub for international banking, which is just the other side of the River Lea. Regeneration is most often gentrification, and London Docklands is no exception. The old working-class community of former dock workers was largely displaced and is now dwarfed by the professional classes moving in. Britannia Village is increasingly comprised of short-term let apartments, especially along the dock, with new 'gated communities' springing up along the banks of the Thames, housing commuters from the finance sector. With wealth and poverty cheek-by-jowl, crime was a problem. The ward had among the worst per capita crime rates in the borough and lacked community facilities and any sense of community cohesion.

My first impression when I drove into the area was that it looked like a film set. Where were all the people? It seemed that community had been 'planned out' of the urban village. The flats and town houses had no front gardens to meet neighbours and the communal green was landscaped to prevent children playing football on it. There was a tangible socio-economic divide. The road the church manse stood on ran through the centre of the 'village'. On one side was social housing, on the other, private flats and growing gated communities.

In 2007 Penny announced she was moving on after nine years of digging prayerful foundations in that community, starting a local charity and planting the seeds of a local church. Royal Docks Community Church was a small congregation of twelve adults, and not all local people. There was no stipend, no church building, but with great foresight, the London Baptist Association had purchased a four-bedroom townhouse as a manse in the middle of the development. It was large enough to host gatherings of around fifteen people. When Penny said it was time to move on, Dave knew he was called to take over. The only thing that stood in the way was our lifelong commitment to Bonny Downs, our three teenage children who would resent even the idea of moving out of the family circle in East Ham, and me. Mostly he was afraid of telling me.

When he did, I believe I heard the truth being spoken. My acceptance was more 'this will happen' than any sense of wanting it to. I knew Dave was speaking the truth: God wanted us to move and take over the work at Britannia Village. We both knew it would not be easy.

Hearing harsh realities

And then we met our Agabus. Agabus is the person who tells you the cold, hard truth about what lies ahead in God's plan. In Acts 21, Agabus used visual aids to get his point across: shackling Paul's hands and feet he prophesied that a season of persecution was coming. If you are an Agabus prophet, you won't expect a round of applause. It's not a comfortable message to give. It's not a comfortable message to hear. As we prepared to move to the Royal Docks we met our Agabus. Colin Marchant is a seasoned Baptist minister, now retired; a former president of the Baptist Union. He had joined Bonny Downs some years earlier and had been writing an academic paper looking at the 'Faith Flows' in Newham, from the earliest Christian settlement until the present day. We confided in him our sense of call to the Docks and Colin told us the hard truth. There had never been a church lasting more than one generation in West Silvertown. Many denominations had tried and all had failed. One after another, in one generation, around 40 years, they were gone. The revivals which had invigorated other parts of Newham, left the spiritual landscape of the area south of the Docks untouched. Methodist, Pentecostal and earlier Baptist plants all failed. The Anglican Church building at St Marks had been turned into a somewhat bawdy music hall, a monument to the old-time East End culture which had rapidly evaporated from the gentrified streets around.

And still we knew it was true: we would go. What is more, we knew we needed to work in reverse. Where Bonny Downs had been a small church which grew a community project, West Silvertown would be a community development project which might, we hoped, one day give birth to a sustainable, local, inclusive, enduring church. It was just that it seemed impossible. Seeking comfort, and with Colin's insight ringing in our ears, we spoke to a number of other local ministers and prayer walkers.

'It's like building a pyramid with marbles,' said one such Agabus.

'There's something poisoned in the spiritual soil,' said another.

'You have heard of spiritual "thin places? Silvertown is a 'thick place".'

We were meeting Agabus at every turn and the wisdom of family and friends was not to leave the fruits of ministry in East Ham that we loved, and go to such an unpromising place.

We went.

Missional community

It was after we committed to go that God's plan started to be revealed. The first confirmation came when Dave was offered a job running Britannia Village Hall. This community centre was managed by East Thames Housing Group, the very institution he had left to pursue ministry in the 1990s. This meant we had a wage and a foothold in community life. I was then offered a temporary contract at a local university, teaching sociology. As the year turned to 2008 we moved our very reluctant children into the manse at 20 Gatcombe Road and started a new episode of 'finding Lydia'. We were out of our depth from day one.

The first three years were a transition. Like others called to uncharted waters, we spent a good deal of time listening to people and watching our community, taking its pulse. We closed the Sunday worship service. It was just too weird having ten people gather by sitting in rows on Sunday. The small congregation was encouraged to worship in other local fellowships, some going over to Bonny Downs, while we scoped the land to see where God was already at work. Instead, small midweek groups met in the manse, over meals, and slowly we started to see tentative steps ahead.

We discerned that loving the hell out of this area would involve showing what God's Kingdom looked like locally: tackling injustice and focussing on celebrating the assets we had as a community. This is a method used by community developers called ABCD[19]. Rather than focussing on deficits, the things a community lacks, or seeking answers outside the community, asset-based approaches look for existing, often under-used, assets *within* the community, however 'deprived' it might have been labelled. It seeks to empower and encourage people to use their skills and gifts to effect positive change for themselves. It usually involves linking people together to mobilise action. It may involve bringing in resources from outside to work alongside local initiatives, but it avoids doing things 'for' people. The opposite, 'deficit approach', focusses on what is lacking, what is broken. It often ends up doing things 'to' deprived communities. This can, at best, only provide temporary change and can lead to longer term disempowerment and entrenched disadvantage as local people accept the narrative that they are powerless and need help.[20] ABCD holds to the idea

---

[19] http://altogetherbetter.org.uk/Data/Sites/1/5assetbasedcommunitydevelopment. pdf for an explanation and list of ABCD resources.

[20] Robert D. Lupton (2012) *Toxic Charity: How Churches and Charities Hurt Those They Help (And How to Reverse It)*

that communities can drive their own development. In Biblical terms, it's the 'loaves and fishes' story. It's when a group of Jesus' disciples, overwhelmed by the need around them, perhaps already tired and wishing the crowd would disappear, hear Jesus say, 'You feed them' (Matthew 14:16). It seems ridiculous. It is of course, impossible. But, looking round for what they have, they make a start, and end up feeding a multitude with the equivalent of a child's 'Happy Meal'.

Within months of Dave being commissioned as the new minister of Royal Docks Community Church, we saw the danger of taking a 'churchy' approach to seeking God's Kingdom in the Royal Docks. We could easily get consumed by the demands of trying to maintain a worship meeting, while the needs and Kingdom potential in the area were left untouched. Closing the formal Sunday worship services had opened up spaces to meet in new ways. Our gatherings were open meals, and the Royal Docks Community Church mantra of 'we don't meet unless we eat' was emerging. Church was around a table. Our neighbours were invited.

'I♡BV'

Dave's intuition was to begin to change the narrative about Britannia Village, from a place with problems and divisions to a place which was loved and cared for. We started in earnest in the first summer of 2008. Dave decided to invest six weeks of the school holidays in running a youth project in an attempt to stem the tide of crime. It was called, in a flagrant counterfeiting of New York's slogan, 'I♡BV'. There was no funding and no personnel. Undeterred, Dave had a stack of T-shirts printed and started to chat to local teenagers, offering them work helping to run a summer scheme for younger kids. Funding had not been secured, but a summer of crime was the last thing the community needed. Our own children helped and took part.[21] Around 80 local children came every day for six weeks. There was no other youth provision in the neighbourhood and most families had no other childcare options. We began to get to know neighbouring families in a very real way, spending day after day in Britannia Village Hall and on the village green. At first, some of the professional community were wary of all this youth activity, but at the end of the summer the ward's crime rates were released and they were won over. In the summer of 2008, West Silvertown had fallen from its notorious

---

[21] The picture on the 'Looking for Lydia' tab www.bonnydownschurch.org is of our daughter Lizi, then 16, volunteering on the summer scheme at BV.

place at the top of the borough's crime ratings. The quarterly crime figures usually doubled in the summer months, but in July-September 2008, in BV, they had halved. The local police sergeant said that our youthwork met three quarters of the anti-crime strategy in the area. By the end of the summer we were exhausted, but a pattern had been set. The Kingdom of God could be seen in this place. We had made friends with many families and won support from the private tenants' associations. We had begun. We measured church growth by the reduction in the crime rate.

In the following years a funded youth worker, Steve Allgood, was appointed and community workers from BDCA were seconded to help build on these early foundations. A key part of how we began to impact the area without exhausting ourselves was to welcome a series of young interns. They were all unpaid, housed with us in the manse or with another local woman who remained part of the church from the original congregation. Our fresh-faced interns arrived on gap years, and many have stayed long after, including Helen our first intern, who arrived in 2009. It took some explaining that while she had come to undertake a church placement, we did not have Sunday worship, but took local people on 'mission trips' to Romania; a church which did not have formal members, but met over meals and ran weekly breakfasts in the community hall; which did not really know what it was doing, but would do whatever it could to show love and bring justice to the Royal Docks. Helen fell in love with West Silvertown and felt a call to the area which matched the one we had felt at Bonny Downs years before. She changed her university plans and stayed local, stepping into the church leadership team. Years later she married Donald Fernandes, a man equally committed to the neighbourhood and willing to live communally. Today, Helen is the associate minister of Royal Docks Community Church and she and Donald live in the shared house at Gatcombe Road. Helen will step up to replace us when our transition from Senior Leadership ends in a few years' time.

One valuable resource to guide our efforts as the wisdom of Robert Linthicum. His book *Building a People of Power: Equipping Churches to Transform Their Communities* (2006) helped us avoid the traps of doing things 'to' or 'for' people in marginalised communities and seek ways to empower change from locals themselves. Linthicum taught us that finding local 'Carers, Connectors, Guards and Gossips' was invaluable in community development. Right from the start we met these 'Lydias' in Britannia Village, people from surprising quarters who could see what we were attempting and opened doors for us and shared the load. Some found faith. All, we believe, got a taste of the Kingdom.

Leaning into faith and each other

Reflecting on the early years at Britannia Village, we are pleased that we were told the truth about West Silvertown. It is a demanding place to minister, hard ground to plant in. Several times in the first few years either Dave or I would feel overwhelmed by the intractable problems and the 'spiritual heaviness' of the place. At these times, one of us wanted to leave, to return to things we knew and a community with better resources to counter its problems. But we never felt this at the same time. We would be each other's 'Silas' at these times, singing worship in the darkest times to encourage the other to carry on. (In Acts 16:16-40, Paul and Silas worship in prison together) We downloaded Maggi Dawn's song, 'I will wait for your peace to come to me' with its words, 'I'll sing in the darkness and wait without fear'. When we felt useless and ineffective we played this song and reminded each other of the clarity of God's call which had so surprisingly brought us there. We stayed. We sold our house in Bonny Downs to my brother and his wife, who would herself become a leader at Bonny Downs Church. We dug in and clung on.

Colonial legacy

We discerned that the unhealthy spiritual atmosphere, which had been so graphically described to us, could not be countered by separating out worship from justice. Perhaps the roots of the Docklands' spiritual poverty lay in its role in colonial exploitation decades before? Goods looted from the Empire passed through the Royal Docks, bringing incredible wealth to the elite, but leaving the average dock worker with a precarious income and the likelihood of an early death from work-related accidents. The average life expectancy of a working man in the Royal Docks at the turn of the 20th century was 29 years old, even less than the gas and chemical workers along the Thames at Beckton. Men were made to vie for work at the dock gates; only the fittest were chosen for the jobs available that day. There were always men sent away. The Great Dock Strike in 1889 brought national attention to the scandalous exploitation of the dock community; Karl Marx's daughter was a leading organiser. It seemed to us that the history of global and local exploitation, and the dependency culture which arose from poverty, were at the roots of the spiritual heaviness of the neighbourhood. Our era of gentrification only compounded the narrative. One half of the community was hearing, 'you are not wanted, you are dispensable', while the professional incomers felt disconnected from the area's history and afraid of their neighbours: dislocation and isolation. If the spiritual ground was poisoned, it could not be addressed by church planting that did not tackle injustice and empower local people.

'Anti-terror cells'

Our church planting years in the Docks began with an intention to tell a different version of the local narrative, to speak a new story. 'I♡BV' was not just a good idea socially, it was our first public prophetic storytelling. Our community *could* rise to meet its own challenges. It just needed a dose of audacious faith. The early BV years also confirmed the lessons learnt at BDCA. In order to become relevant, and be more than a shrinking religious club, the church needed to leave behind the idea that 'just doing the same things, only better' would break the spiritual apathy and mistrust of church in the inner city, especially among the white working class. Not having a church building was a gift; it forced us to adopt a different stance. We were a small Christian community. We were not powerful. We were not resourced. We needed to make use of shared, community spaces and we would focus on expressing the truths and hopes of the Kingdom message Jesus preached. Missiology would shape ecclesiology, or in other words, the gathered Christian community was first and foremost a missional group, called together to work as 'anti-terror cells' in our neighbourhood. Over many meals and midweek gatherings, we plotted ways to challenge the brokenness and celebrate the beauty of our neighbourhood. We read the Bible with neighbours who had never heard its stories, and this brought them to life. We would share more and more of our lives (more about living communally in these years later). All this activity led to new reflection on Scripture as we inadvertently fell into a Liberation Theology theory of knowledge and learning: sharing insights, and learning by reflecting on doing. Service in our community was the opener for worship. We would sing hymns later - and we do! Sunday worship gatherings began in 2011 and continue to be enjoyed in lively meetings from 5.30pm in Britannia Village Hall.[22]

---

[22] Royal Docks Community Church website is www.royaldockschurche16.com

The early years in the Docks underscored the knowledge that incarnational living and full immersion (we are Baptists after all) into a community's life was a pre-requisite for church planting. As we dug deeper into our faith I felt a call to step out of full-time work and become an accredited minister myself. We lived every day as 'church' and our reluctant teens found their feet more quickly than we had hoped. Both our daughters met their husbands in those years, and today both couples serve in the fellowship worshipping at Royal Docks Community Church. Just like the early years of BDCA, we had no idea what to do, but some good principles to follow. We began outside of the institution of Sunday church and began by looking for Lydia in our community. And we met her in many surprising ways.

Some questions to reflect on...
*This chapter mentions an 'asset' rather than 'deficit' model of community development. Can you identity the under-used **assets** in your community which might be harnessed for its transformation? Have you sought wisdom from others as you seek to live out a sense of calling? What if they tell you some **harsh realities**? The beginning of our time at RDCC can be described as **mission** fully shaping the life of the church...can you see how this focus might disrupt, and provide space, for new ways of being church in your context? How would you feel about this?*

4. RECOGNISING CORNELIUS

Acts 10:28 Peter told them, 'You know it is against our laws for a Jewish man to enter a Gentile home like this or to associate with you. But God has shown me that I shall no longer think of anyone as impure or unclean.'

Something else happens when Christians lose some of their 'churchianity'. They start to recognise Cornelius; the person who breaks down prejudice.

Peter was a good Jew and a Christian leader. He could quote Levitical laws and had kept them all his life. But, as he followed his call to be a 'fisher of men' something began tugging at the edges of his identity as part of a 'separate race'. At that time, Gentile converts had to accept the customs and initiation rites of Judaism as part of their conversion to Christianity. The original Jewish disciples saw Gentiles as ritually unclean. Their Scriptures were clear about this, forbidding social contact in all meaningful ways. The Gentiles were there to be taught the better ways of the Jews. If they heard the Gospel of Jesus and responded to it, they needed to meet the norms of the Jewish majority in the Church before they could be welcomed: get circumcised; keep Kosher. And then Peter has a dream. God shows him all the symbols of Gentile uncleanliness and says, 'Don't call unclean what I call clean'. He wakes and there are Gentiles at his door.

It took the first church many heated debates and a Council in Jerusalem before they could cross ethnic divides and see Gentiles as fully equal disciples of Jesus. But it wasn't actually debates which opened the door of Gentile inclusion. Encounters did. It was the experience of meeting the 'Other' and seeing that the Spirit was at work in them. That is what it took to nudge the early Church along towards inclusion.

There was a time when the Bible was used to condone the enslavement of Africans. It was the almost universal opinion among Western Christianity that God had ordained slavery, and clergymen had no qualms about owning slaves themselves. It never occurred to them that slave trading might be immoral. The most famous English slave trader, Sir John Hawkins, named his slave ships 'Angel', 'Jesus' and 'Grace of God'. In time, Western Christians would be challenged to rethink their ideas of 'race' and drop colonial attitudes to Black and Minority Ethnic communities (they haven't achieved this yet). In my lifetime the Church would be challenged to drop its exclusion of women from ministry roles (ditto). Countering prejudice with the words 'God has shown me that I shall no longer think of anyone as impure or unclean' has been a long, slow arc towards inclusion. It began when Peter met Cornelius, when Philip met an Ethiopian eunuch, when Paul met many Lydias; in other words, when the Church got missional. There's much to say to explain this, and I know the well-rehearsed arguments of those who want to defend the 'Us and Them' identity of Christianity. These debates are for another time. Here, I want to talk about the principle of recognising Cornelius, the person who challenges your prejudice, which is part of the story we lived. You won't drop your prejudices unless you are open to such encounters too.

Our Cornelius encounters

The greatest Cornelius in our lives was my best friend Vaughan. We met as undergraduates and formed a connection that would surprise us, and some others, but would be the best friendship of my life. On paper, we had nothing in common. Vaughan was from an upper middle class, ex-pat family; well educated, West London living, cultured and High Catholic. I was a working class, East End mother of three from a low-church background. Vaughan attended Tridentine Latin Masses in the West End. My Baptist church was what he described as a 'Church of Casseroles'. He would take me to the Oratory, and I was wowed by the beauty and sense of transcendence. I took him to Bonny Downs and he was shocked by the raw honesty. Vaughan was gay. Growing up he had been told by Evangelical Christians that he was an abomination and damned to hell. You would have expected him to give me a wide berth. He got over his prejudices. He crossed the dividing line and we laughed our way through our university years and for decades to come. His wit was a match for my East End gab. He opened up a new world of culture to me. I shared my family life with him, inviting him to live with us when his health took a turn for the worse, and the busyness of my family distracted him from his own pain. There is so much I could tell you about this remarkable man and his partner Robbie, who had been with him for longer than Dave and I had been married. When Vaughan and Robbie celebrated their civil partnership after over twenty years of life together, they chose just two guests, two Baptist ministers, me and Dave, as witnesses. And then we feasted on fish and chips and champagne. For the purpose of this story Vaughan was a true Cornelius.

I had been raised by Christian parents who were horrified at the casual homophobia in the Christian culture surrounding them. They practised generous love and were anti-prejudice in every sense. This gave me a good foundation on which to work out my own theology of inclusion. Christians in the West find ourselves living within in a culture fixated with sex. Unfortunately, the Church's response has been too often to turn to scapegoating; homophobia is coming out of the Church closet. LGBT+ inclusion has become a fundamental issue. This is a great shame and says more about what the Church wants to keep in the closet: its own lack of integrity in sexual ethics. It says far less about a proper consideration of the passages used to weaponise Scripture and exclude those it deems 'unclean'. Meeting Vaughan, and seeing the love between him and Robbie, sent me back to the 'clobber' passages in my Bible. I educated myself, and when I was sure that the Church had been as wrong to be complicit in homophobia as it had been in its use of African slaves and its exclusion of women leaders like myself, I joined the organisation 'Accepting Evangelicals'. I started to give seminars explaining my interpretation of these passages in Scripture.

The Church needs a dream like Peter's in Acts 10: a revelation to tear apart prejudice and reshape who it sees as 'impure and unclean'. And thank God, it seems, some are having it. But on the whole, sadly, Christians won't stop talking about an 'issue' and start meeting Cornelius; the person who might help challenge their prejudice.

Vaughan was not the only gay man who would challenge prejudice for us. Dave's first and best ally in tackling the unmet needs and structural injustices in Britannia Village was a local councillor, Steve Brayshaw. Steve and Dave started walking their dogs around Lyle Park on Sunday mornings, sharing ways they could encourage community cohesion and improve life in Britannia Village. Steve had two lively basset hounds. Dave walked my Shih-Zhou. We later found out that some locals assumed Dave and Steve were partners because of these Sunday morning walks. They were! They were Kingdom collaborators conspiring for the common good of an area they loved and were committed to. Dave worked at this from his faith, Steve from his politics. Steve was not just a good contact to work with, but showed a genuine concern for Dave when he exhausted himself. He was a wise counsellor as well as a great local councillor.

The Corneliuses kept coming. Having deconstructed any sense of 'otherness' among our gay neighbours, God took to tackling another potential prejudice – against Tories! Dave's next ally in running the local charity that managed Britannia Village Hall was a man who had stood against Steve Brayshaw in the local election, Neil Pearce, a member of the Conservative Party. Working for the common good was truly shaking the billboards of prejudice.

Homophobia and political allegiances are not the only prejudices which might be shaken loose by living in a missional community. The next Cornelius challenged some of the latent 'Messiah Complex' that can be picked up by those who work with the homeless.

Angie's God-dream

While we were putting down roots in the Dock community, my sister Angela Allgood was being kept awake at night back in the church at Bonny Downs. A trained social worker and experienced community developer, Angie was feeling more than a little stirred about the rising levels of poverty and homelessness in East Ham. She was working for BDCA in the Children and Families team but it was the homeless and the hungry that were filling her mind at night. Looking up a passage on fasting for her son's homework, Angie stumbled on Isaiah 58 talking about the 'true fast' God requires – 'Is it not to share your food with the hungry and to provide the poor wanderer with shelter – when you see the naked, to clothe them?' She could not shake it. Angie was serving on the leadership team at Bonny Downs and shared her sense that God was asking the church to do something about this. It was not a comfortable meeting and began an unsettling time for her. Perhaps the church at Bonny Downs was gravitating away from seeking justice – after all, wasn't that what the much larger charity BDCA did? Bonny Downs Church had become more concerned with 'spiritual' things. Angie could not let it go.

Anyone who knows what holy discontent feels like might wish less for a calling. It can be very troubling, especially when the need for action is not fully supported by your church leaders. But Angie persisted. She knew God would not let her excuse herself by saying, 'They didn't listen.' God might not have been speaking to her church leaders at Bonny Downs about this. But God was clearly saying it, night after sleepless night, to her. From these months of wrestling with discontent a thriving Poverty Response Project would be born. Eventually it formed into a new branch of BDCA and today Angie's project is fully at the heart of Bonny Downs Church.

With consent to use the old building, Angie set up a weekly food bank with wraparound advocacy care, a school uniform bank and an open meal for rough sleepers, which has grown to serve around 50 people every Wednesday. While the church had been initially unsure, the community provided keen volunteers and slowly the congregation got on board too. At almost the same time, Jonny, one of the interns at Royal Docks Community Church, living with us at Gatcombe Road, had a similar dream to start a winter night shelter in Newham. Jonny had left a prestigious career in Formula 1 and a leafy village in Cambridgeshire to come and take his new-found faith seriously in the inner city. Initially he came for a one-year internship, working in our youth club. God wanted more. Before arriving in London, Jonny had not seen street homelessness. While living in the Docks he started volunteering in a night shelter project in a neighbouring borough and began to float the idea with Angie that the churches in Newham could do something similar. This is how God-dreams start. Someone has a sense that, not only is something wrong, but that God wants something done about it. Angie was Jonny's 'Ananias-encourager' Although he had no experience in social work or any prior track record in running a Christian ministry, Angie backed Jonny. The NewWay night shelter has been running for five years now. 384 guests have been housed for the winter months in Newham churches – a total of 598 safe nights–with a hot meal, breakfast and advocacy advisors provided. 123 street sleepers have been helped into permanent accommodation and 89 into temporary accommodation. A total of 16 churches have stepped up to host what is now a five month programme with a three-day-a-week day centre all year round hosted in the Bobby Moore Pavilion.[23]

Dropping the Messiah complex

Having so many homeless people in the midweek life of the church facilitated many other opportunities to meet Cornelius – the person who challenges prejudice. One of the food bank's first guests, Dave Quinn, has been this for me. Dave's life has been beset by post-traumatic stress after leaving the armed forces, which led to alcoholism and homelessness. Yet his faith shines through the brokenness of his life - but only if you drop the need to 'fix Dave'. Dave makes tea every Sunday for the congregation at Bonny Downs and is the keenest volunteer in the Food Bank. Dave and another homeless friend collect the free food from local bakeries and supermarkets which feeds our guests every Wednesday. Rain or shine, Dave and his trolley trek up and down East Ham High Street collecting food that would otherwise be thrown away but which Terri at the foodbank will turn into a meal for 50.

Sometimes Dave worships with us in the evening service at Royal Docks Community Church. One Sunday the invitation to take communion had left me glued to my seat. For whatever reason, I was feeling empty and low and could not get myself to the table. Head down, I was 'sitting it out'. Then I felt a touch on my shoulder and there was Dave Quinn, bread and wine in his hand. 'This is for you. I think you need it.' Dave served me and prayed for me. He may have been a little drunk. He was also completely tuned into God. I don't think anyone else has ever brought me communion before or since. Dave Quinn taught me that no-one is someone primarily to be 'fixed'. St John of the Cross is right. The cracks let the light in. When we encounter 'the poor', not as some homogenous group of 'the homeless' but as real people, people like Dave, they can become Cornelius to us.

Speaking at the five-year celebration for NewWay, Jonny said, 'working with NewWay has shown me how to take my mask off. I am broken too, just like the people I advocate for. But they don't wear masks and have shown me how to take mine off'. Who knew? A high-flying F1 man needed to meet Cornelius in the guise of street sleepers in the East End. They broke through the sense of entitlement and perfectionism which was destroying

---

[23] NewWay website https://www.newwayproject.org/

his soul. And a minister needed to be given communion by a homeless man.

Dave Quinn and the many homeless people who are part of our faith community have helped us to break down our prejudices. Homelessness can happen to anyone. Our society placates its guilt by insisting poverty is due to personal deficiency, a lack of character or the result of bad decisions. At best, the stories of the poor are cast as unavoidable tragedies. At worst, we hold those at the margins up to ridicule and social shame. Encountering the guests at NewWay teaches us that there are more fundamental, structural reasons for the dramatic rise in street sleeping. Political decisions to prioritise building unaffordable housing and to offer 'flexible' work contracts have pushed many people into precarious living – we live among what Guy Standing calls The Precariat[24]. This is compounded by a Department of Work and Pensions which sanctions benefits first, and resolves cases slowly. Our food bank and night shelter are full of Corneliuses who will challenge our prejudices about 'the homeless', but you need to meet them and listen to their stories and not just do good 'to' them. Angie's obedience has blessed our congregations with many possible encounters. Today she dreams of when the Poverty Response Project is not needed.

A Muslim angel Gabriel

One more story, and one more strange Cornelius. This one is about the Muslim Angel Gabriel. With Angie leading the way, others at Bonny Downs were learning once again to 'blur the edges' of church life. Other dreams of breaking out of 'churchianity' were being formed. There are lots of them. This is just one more.

Stacey Cordery and Sarah Laing, who lead the Children and Families team at BDCA are also church leaders at Bonny Downs. They live and breathe inclusion and have a passion to bring the multi-everything community in East Ham together. To this end they help organise celebrations of 'Eid and Diwali as well as Easter in BDCA's community garden, and find common ground in supporting local parents to raise their children together. Working for a community charity and serving their church passionately, they wear their dual hats well. Sometimes this duality gives rise to surprising projects.

---

[24] Guy Standing (2011) *The Precariat: The New Dangerous Class*, Bloomsbury Press

As Christmas approached, they hit on the idea of bringing together the way the church would celebrate and the potential for community involvement. They invited all the BDCA families to take part in a community nativity play that would be performed at the church's Nativity Service on the Sunday before Christmas - after a month of weekly after-school sessions to rehearse, learn songs and make scenery and props. The idea was a success. They found the Muslim and Hindu parents were actually relieved that religion was respected and that their children were included in a tradition they valued. So every week, out came the Gospels, on went the tea towels, and the birth of Jesus was retold in the community. Nativity Sunday was packed. It was standing room only. The multi-faith cast brought their families to applaud the cute angels and cheeky animals and an errant Christmas star, who, overwhelmed by the crowd, had a stellar meltdown. The Angel Gabrielle's Muslim family were taken aback with the welcome, and everyone stayed to chat and eat mince pies. Of course we did, it was Christmas. Wasn't the original Nativity story a tale of God refusing to stick to ethnic and religious divisions? Wouldn't the first shepherd-witnesses have been excluded from the Temple on grounds of their cultural impurity? Weren't the Magi there to honour the child, despite their foreign religion and star-gazing ways? The Nativity story is one great 'blurry edge' encounter. It is full of Corneliuses.

Blurry edge church

Missional community life has not diluted the Gospel one bit. But it has helped shake off the prejudices which bolster a 'Christian' identity which defines itself by a system of exclusionary practices and looks so unlike Jesus himself. This false identity finds security in setting up lines between 'pure' and 'impure' and is toxic and hateful to 'others'. It also bends out of shape those within its structures. As we reflect on our experience of Church, we are sad to say that we have been raised in a Christian culture which formulates its identity by drawing up boundaries between 'Us' and 'Them'. The Church has been imagined to be a 'bounded set', with all kinds of ways to draw distinctions between insiders and outsiders; even Christians from other denominations have been seen as outsiders! Our journey has challenged this was of thinking. Today, our experience of 'being Church' has far less distinct edge: no longer a 'bounded set', it has become, for us, a community centred on Christ. We have begun to see that everyone journeying towards Jesus belongs to each other. We are still finding ways to break down the barriers and we speak of 'blurry edge church' to describe the community ministries which characterise our congregational life. It's a change of mind-set. It's repentance.

Peter met Cornelius and became a better follower of Jesus. Our journey has been full of opportunities to do the same.

Some questions to reflect on ...

*I suggest here that 'experiences of **alterity'** – how we are changed by meaningful encounters with people we might have been taught to avoid - have been important in how we understand the reach of the Gospel. Is this true of your journey? Who are your **Corneliuses**?*

This chapter retold stories from our adventures outside of 'churchianity'. Do you have similar stories to tell?

*We spoke about how we need to be freed from the idea that some people are primarily in our lives to be '**fixed'**. Have you been blessed by seeing Jesus present in the messy brokenness of life in your community?*

*We suggest that the 'Us and Them' bounded-set way of seeing church requires repentance. What would a '**Christ-centred'** approach look like in your community or church? What would start to shake loose from structures and practices if your current boundaries were blurred?*

5. STANDING UP TO FELIX, FESTUS AND AGRIPPA

Acts 25:6-7 After spending eight or ten days with them, Festus went down to Caesarea. The next day he convened the court and ordered that Paul be brought before him. When Paul came in, the Jews who had come down from Jerusalem stood round him. They brought many serious charges against him but they could not prove them.

In Paul's day, power structures were layered and complicated. There was a struggle for authority and a desire to shift responsibility, particularly where it interfered with political agendas. Paul found himself in the tangle of political webs many times. In Acts 23-25 he has a series of run-ins with the Roman Governors, Felix and Festus, and the puppet King Agrippa. For several years he is passed between them as they attempt to find the most expedient way to deal with this 'troublemaker'. The Bible account contains a good deal of irony. The more those in power feel they have the upper hand, the more, through patience and faith, Paul prevails, winning his right to an audience in Rome with Caesar himself.

Community organisers often find themselves at odds with those who hold statutory power. Britannia Village gave many opportunities to meet our own Felixes, Festuses and Agrippas.

Village politics

Britannia Village is a political place. When Dave arrived to manage the village hall there were already many layers of power. Although it has only 1,400 homes, Britannia Village is split between 12 management companies and two social landlords. The original developers were required to build a community centre, and continued to exert their influence in the foundation that had been set up to develop the local community. The developers had economic interests in keeping down the running costs of Britannia Village Hall, which led to the strange situation where the hall was largely unused. Penny, the original church planter, had battled for many years to lease a small space in which to offer community activities. It was always at significant cost. When Dave arrived, control of the hall had been transferred to a local charity but the developers' influence continued. This led to a number of run-ins where Dave's desire to fill the hall with local people, and to give them a better say at management levels, ran counter to others' desires to keep costs down and manage risk. By the end of 2009 Dave was barred from entering the building he managed! Perhaps this was done in the hope that he would resign, but those taking this decision were unaware that there are plenty of Biblical models to follow when facing up to Felix, Festus and Agrippa. Dave spent three months confined to a desk off-site, where he surreptitiously managed the Village Hall by phone and sought ways to change the balance of power. By changing faces and winning hearts on the board, Dave was welcomed back with new freedom and a new mandate to use the hall for community transformation in 2010.

Reflecting on this experience, we have come to know that it's not our role to seek confrontation. However, not being intimidated, being willing to be patient and ready to stand up for what is right are essential in community development. Today the board of trustees managing the centre is entirely comprised of local people. They are a diverse group and bring a wealth of skills and experience. This board has been chaired in turn by our good friend and local Labour councillor Steve Brayshaw, and later by the Conservative candidate Neil Pearce. To date, this local charity has successfully brought in a GP surgery and a local day-care nursery into BV. They helped parents set up their own After School Club and raised money to provide a Multi-Use Games Area on the Village Green. The Village Hall hosts twice weekly toddler groups, free English classes, a community breakfast, two nights of youth work and many sports and fitness classes. Dave continues to work one day a week in community development at Britannia Village alongside Helen Fernandes, our church's associate minister, who was successfully appointed to be the new Community Development Worker in 2017.

Youthwork

There were others holding power in Britannia Village. There were a good number of young people who exerted their authority through crime and drug dealing. At times, Dave lived with the threat of violence. Persistence and patience paid off here too. One event helped to change some of the suspicion these young people had about Dave's role in the community. Leaving the hall one night, Dave witnessed a group of young people being aggressively 'stopped and searched' by the Territorial Support Group - a police team from outside the area. He intervened to challenge what was happening and to calm the situation. This happened a number of times. On one occasion Dave discovered a police sergeant had been distributing political propaganda among the private residents. Dave challenged this but was accused, in a public meeting, of lying. It was time to stand up to Felix again. Dave took out a formal complaint, which led to this officer being reprimanded and transferred out of the area. These battles helped save the relationship between Dave and local young people from being adversarial. He would never condone criminal behaviour but would always stand up against the injustices they experienced.

Through years of youth work, led by a man who must win the award for the world's most resilient youth leader - Steve Allgood - we always tried to give young people a voice within their own community. This included hosting a number of community conversations in Britannia Village. One of these brought together local young people and private residents who were concerned about crime. Listening to each other and learning each other's names made it easier not to scapegoat and to understand each other's perspectives.

Youth work is a long-term slog. Often it is thankless, and in our society it is massively under-resourced and undervalued. We could not have countered the power of youth crime without Steve Allgood's amazing commitment and the input of our gap year interns. Dave's willingness to engage with young people eventually won us many friends. Ironically, the only boy who ever physically attacked Dave would become one of the few to join the worship gatherings years later.

Public Baptisms

Power can be challenged in other ways. There is a great deal to be said for counter-cultural displays which intrigue rather than confront. We found many ways to do this. One of the most fun was to hold public baptisms. We have baptised six people in the Royal Victoria Dock, two in the River Thames and two women in a park lake.

We baptised Jonny Adams and Donald Fernandes during the 2012 Summer Olympics. The ExCeL exhibition centre, a venue opposite Britannia Village, was used for some of the indoor events and so the dockside was heaving with tourists. We handed out leaflets that said 'Don't worry, we aren't drowning them, we are baptising them!' with a short testimony from Jonny and Donald on the back. The youth group jumped in as Jonny was baptised and swam around him chanting his name. The church had a picnic and sang songs on the side of the Dock. In later years, when we were warned off using the Dock as a baptistery, we jumped a fence in the local park to baptise our own son Mikey and his cousin Joe in the Thames at high tide and in the pouring rain on Easter Sunday. During that service, one action came to represent what all these intriguing public demonstrations were about. Dave drove a wooden stake into the ground and said, 'We stake our claim on this area for the Kingdom of God'.[25]

Education Opportunities

Life in Britannia Village involved living among an ever-changing population. One reason for this was that many families left the area when their children approached secondary school age. The local primary school had successfully been steered from 'special measures' to 'outstanding' within 18 months by the inspirational head teacher Linda-May Bingham, a Christian woman from a neighbouring borough. Newham secondary schools face the challenges of a massive young population, high levels of transfer as the population churns, and the challenges of poverty. In

---

[25] There are photos of our dock baptisms on the 'Looking for Lydia' tab on www.bonnydownschurch.org tab and on the Royal Docks Community Church website www.royaldockschurch16.com

general, secondary schools in Newham are huge with 1,500-2,000 pupils, and have sometimes been seen as failing and dangerous places for aspirational families to send their children. Our three children were educated in local schools so we know that some of this was a misrepresentation and driven by fear. However, although today many are out-performing similar schools, when we arrived in the Docks the local school had a GCSE pass rate of just 33%, which meant the majority of locally-educated children left school at 16 with less than five passes at GCSE.

Dave quickly realised that youth work could only scratch the surface of the needs of young people. Good education, which provided aspiration and confidence, was needed to keep families in the area, and provide positive alternatives to crime. In 2007, Dave and Linda-May began to discuss bidding to open a smaller, local, secondary school for Britannia Village. The first bid to Newham council was unsuccessful. As legislation changed and the new free school movement allowed local groups to bid directly to central government they submitted three further bids to the Department for Education, all unsuccessfully. Resilience pays off when dealing with political power. In 2012 a new submission was made for an Academy School in Silvertown, in partnership with Oasis Community Learning, and it was successful! The temporary school would be housed in the Village Hall, would open to a maximum of 90 pupils per year, and a new, purpose-designed building would be constructed on the site of the old West Silvertown fire station. This short paragraph brushes over years of battles and many apparently insurmountable obstacles. And yet the school is open, and building work on the new site is due to begin soon. See http://www.oasisacademysilvertown.org/

Structural sin and the reach of the Gospel

Why this focus on schools, crime rates, trustee groups and charities? In the same way that living in a missional community has convinced us that salvation is far more than an individual's experience it has convinced us that sin too is more than personal; it is structural.

The 'Social Gospel' has often been charged with ignoring the central tenets of sin and salvation. This is unfair. It is truer to say that missional living redefines them. Without ignoring the need for personal repentance and the experience of forgiveness, the Kingdom message of Jesus has a broader scope. Human sin infects social structures, oppressing the poor and marginalising the weak. Politics can be used to contain the worst effects of the unfair distribution of power and resources, but we came to see that it is the 'ordinary radicals' of the Kingdom who have the best opportunity to subvert it. This is not primarily through protest, although our story tells us there is a place for confronting injustice this way, but it is more effective and long-lasting when small acts of love and mercy are our tools.

In the story of Acts, Felix, Festus and Agrippa had the power to coerce, to enforce their will on others: this is Weber's classic sociological definition of power. Their power was conferred from an Empire which must have appeared unstoppable. It gave them confidence to treat others, like Paul, as political pawns in their struggle for eminence. But Paul had the power of subversive influence. He had the stronger story. Paul's confidence was in the power of a Kingdom announced by a man dying on a Cross. Jesus exercised power in a truly subversive way: the power of non-violence; of faithful trust in God; of self-emptying love, 'even to death on a cross'. (Philippians 2: 8). There are times when God's people, following God's plans, look to have lost. But love, planted anywhere, never really dies. As Jesus himself demonstrated, it resurrects. Trust in this has given confidence to many people who seek to subvert the power of oppressors. Martin Luther King Jr. expressed this way:

'Evil may so shape events that Caesar will occupy a palace and Christ a cross, but that same Christ will rise up and split history into A.D. and B.C., so that even the life of Caesar must be dated by his name. Yes, "the arc of the moral universe is long, but it bends toward justice." There is something in the universe which justifies William Cullen Bryant in saying, "Truth crushed to earth will rise again."'[26]

Dr. King isn't arguing for a kind of historical determinism. He is not arguing that there's no need to intervene against injustice, because it all comes right in the end. Not at all. Given the context of the quote, its clear

---

[26] Martin Luther King, Jr. from an article printed in 'The Gospel Messenger' 1958. Dr King puts the final, famous phrase in quotes because he was citing 19th century clergyman Theodore Parker, who first coined it in an abolitionist sermon 'Of Justice and the Conscience' published in 1853

Dr King knows that in this world the powerful may have palaces and the righteous may have crosses. But, when you put Jesus in that frame something incredible is revealed, 'Truth crushed to death will rise again'. The struggle for justice is always worthwhile. Those who struggle for it are always, eventually, on the right side. I love the audaciousness of St John who writes in the book of Revelation that love wins. There is a spiritual and moral battle raging but earthly powers fade. The Kingdom of love is eternal. Revelation puts into so many pictures what is expressed in the saying usually attributed to John Lennon, 'It will all be all right in the end. If it's not all right, it's not the end!' For us, this brings 'confidence in what we hope for and assurance about what we do not see.' (Hebrews 1:11). Christian hope is distinct from wishful thinking because it claims to be based in what Jesus has achieved. That gives it legs for the long haul. We have found that struggles against political apathy or injustice require this dimension of supernatural, audacious hope. Others may say they can fight for justice without this. We have found we cannot.

Some questions to reflect on ...

*There is a risk in seeing Christian life as primarily one of protesting against '**worldly powers**'. There is also a risk in seeing faith as only practiced in a '**spiritual realm**'. Which risk do you most easily fall into? Is there a way you see both working together in your struggles against injustice?*

*Have you considered how the **Christian hope** that love and justice ultimatley win might sustain your momentum in the face of opposition?*

*How might you meditate on Christian hope as part of your **everyday practices**?*

6. LIVING WITH PRISCILLA AND AQUILA

Acts 18: 1-3 After this, Paul left Athens and went to Corinth. There he met a Jew named Aquila, a native of Pontus, who had recently come from Italy with his wife Priscilla, because Claudius had ordered all Jews to leave Rome. Paul went to see them, and because he was a tent maker as they were, he stayed and worked with them.

Who knows if Paul planned to live with Priscilla and Aquila? Was this an intentional move or just a pragmatic decision? Did Paul plan on financially supporting his missional work by joining their tent-making business, or did that just happen? Did he find this a distraction, or a blessing? Paul first met this dynamic couple in Corinth. They planted a church together and hosted it in their shared home. Paul lived and worked with them for at least a year and a half. The partnership worked so well that when Paul left for Ephesus, he took Priscilla and Aquila with him. Again, they used their gift of hospitality to build churches; the Ephesian church met in Priscilla and Aquila's house. Having initially left their home in Rome to escape persecution, they evidently returned there. Paul's later letter to the Roman church has a familiar welcome – 'Greet Priscilla and Aquila, my fellow-workers in Christ Jesus...also greet the church that is in their house' (Romans 16-3-5). These were lifelong friends. Sixteen years after Paul first moved in with them, and now in a Roman prison for the second time, his death at the hands of Nero imminent, Paul again writes to greet them. This would be the last paragraph of the last recorded letter in Paul's life (2 Tim 4:19). He spends it sending greetings to his closest friends.

There is so much to say about this couple. How scandalous and counter-cultural that her name is almost always given first! We feminists love moments like that. Isn't it lovely that they live, work and minister together? You never hear one name without the other. And yet despite, or because of the strength of their marriage, they have space for the single man Paul, and then for a whole church, to share their lives and homes.

Sharing homes and bi-vocational living
Ten years in Britannia Village taught us to take hospitality further than ever, and gave us the gift of bi-vocational ministry. We also discovered that discipleship, especially of leaders, could not be achieved other than by living a great deal of life together. What is amazing to us is that so much of this was completely unplanned on our part. The practices which shaped the years we describe, and the people we have become, were accidental or pragmatic decisions. It's only as we look back that we see we stumbled on a way of life that, globally, Christians are rediscovering: shared living and bi-vocational ministry. They are the markers of a way of life which has the potential to subvert capitalism and individualism, the dangerous and destructive 'patterns of this world' (Romans 12: 2). Some, like Shane Claiborne's 'Simple Way' in Philadelphia are blazing a trail. In our own much smaller way, we were learning the practices of missional community. These would make ministry in the inner city not only possible, but joyful.

Gatcombe Road was our first experience of living in a manse, as Bonny Downs Church didn't have one. 20 Gatcombe Road was the house the London Baptist Union had purchased – there was no church building. This church manse at the Docks had been extended into the loft and had four bedrooms and a large meeting room on the ground floor. As our two daughters married and moved out, it struck us as rather immoral that in the midst of a housing crisis there should be an empty bedroom in a house given for ministry. We had always practiced hospitality in our home in East Ham. Exactly one week after we returned from our honeymoon our first houseguest moved in; a member of our extended family with a young daughter and newborn baby. They had been given appalling and unsuitable accommodation in a bed and breakfast hostel, so we offered them to stay with us until something better came up. That began a life of sporadic shared living in East Ham. Family, friends, members of our youth group and people in need of a bit of time in a family setting all came to live with us, staying for between a few weeks to a couple of years. This was a normal extension of family life for us. I was very used to large groups because in the 1970s my parents had moved my sisters and me into a council-run children's home when they became its house parents. In doing so, they included 13 adolescent girls in our family. We were making small fry efforts compared to them.

Living in a manse took this up a notch. In my dreams, I would like to introduce a policy that manses and vicarages should not have empty bedrooms. It might be hard to persuade the current generation of ministers, but it could be introduced in principle to trainees. We knew that our roomy townhouse manse should not only be full, but should act as a living room for the missional community. As the gatherings grew, and Sunday worship was held in the Village Hall, we maintained our practice of regular meals through midweek meetings. I cooked home-made soup and warm bread for the fortnightly gathering of women who would come to Gatcombe Road. Dave opened 'Doritos' for the men.

Interns move in

First to arrive were the interns. They arrived in waves, some dropped off by anxious parents. Did they blame us for their children making such a foolish decision?! I remember that I felt especially nervous about making a good impression when Jonny's parents were due to drop him off. I laid out the best china and made sandwiches. Then, just as the house looked calm and ready, there was a terrible commotion in the street immediately outside our front door. Two grown women were fighting: attempting to knock each other's heads on the ground, rolling over each other, actually tumbling their way around the roundabout in the middle of the road as neighbours cheered and a car full of their children looked on. We have interrupted fights among young people before, but this was something new. It was terribly loud. And it was minutes before the new intern and his family were due to arrive! I went out and, with my best school teacher's voice, I ordered them to let each other go, bundling one of the women into our house and bringing her children inside. They ate the sandwiches. I offered their mum our bathroom and tried to hurry her through the story of why she had been attempting to brain her niece - yes, her niece! - on my doorstep. Within fifteen minutes I had that family sneaking out the back door and into their car to make an escape. And then Mr. and Mrs. Adams arrived. 'How lovely to meet you, do come in!' We ate cake.

The young interns would come from a variety of parachurch organisations to work alongside us. Having them live with us, or with the one other church family with a spare room in the 'village', was the only way to make this possible. Of the 12 current leaders at Royal Docks Community Church, seven lived with us at some time. House prices in London are dreadful, and soon other church families and young people were sharing accommodation too. Some also shared cars and many took holidays together. Living this way cuts expenses. Many of us could not have pursued our dreams of community work and launched projects like NewWay unless we could count on not having to earn a great deal.

Intentional community has taught me one enduring lesson. You need a dressing gown.

The Dos Santos family

More recently, with only our son still at home, we invited a wonderful church family to move in with us. Helio and Jamile Dos Santos faced a terrible decision, a consequence of the structural sin inherent in our housing market. To remain able to pay the escalating rent for their small local house they would need to give up their vocational university training studying architecture and radiography. This was not only scandalous but might mean that we lost this valuable, wonderful couple from the Dock community. Helio was raised in a Brazilian favela. He brings warmth, dynamism and a great sense of joy to the church and is a fearless and invaluable role model among local young people. Jamile brings women together, is a wonderful mother and now a professional radiographer. We knew immediately that it was right to offer them the opportunity to house-share with us. And what a great decision that proved to be! Sharing with the Dos Santos family blessed not only us, but the whole church and neighbourhood. Helio thinks nothing of barbequing a feast for 40, which he regularly does. He is also unimpressed by the notion that our community is gang-ridden. In his home community, gun violence and murder were an almost daily event. We attended their graduation ceremonies with such pride. They model a commitment to education which shames the systems which almost forced them to remain in short-term, unqualified roles.

After two years of living together we suggested that the church appoint Helio and Jamile into formal roles as Children and Families ministers. Everyone agreed. In 2017 we commissioned them at a ceremony where our former intern Helen was recognised as the associate pastor. This began the process of us stepping out of the Senior Leadership role at Royal Docks Community Church, which we think will be a three year transition.

Having a 'proper job'!

I sometimes wonder what life at the Royal Docks would have been like if there had been a stipend to pay us, a church building to access and a big congregation to look after. It would have been 'churchy'. We probably would never have thought to go. Instead, Dave has always had part-time work in the community, shocking the pastors whose congregations hire the hall by being the one to take care of the building and clean the toilets. Too often the church and its ministers are irrelevant to the life of the community they gather in. The fact that Dave worked right at the heart of the 'village' was a blessing.

Working as a teacher and academic has shaped me in ways traditional ministerial training could not have matched. My bi-vocational roles inform and help each other. Being a university lecturer has improved my abilities as a minister by honing my teaching skills, encouraging me to continue to ask questions and keeping me informed about contemporary debates. In so many ways, teaching sociology prompts the skills of enquiry and questioning that also drive my faith. At university I teach courses in inequality, 'race' and gender. My involvement in a missional community has informed my academic interests in inequality and how best to counter it. In my role as an academic I am able to investigate and write papers on the role of the faith sector in welfare and how holistic communities challenge representations of poverty and policy decisions about how to end it. The Poverty Response projects at BDCA have provided amazing resources for ongoing sociological investigation. I listen to stories from my community and they inform my understanding of life in ways which inform my thinking as a sociologist. Some of my students have taken work placements with Angie, with one now working for NewWay as a homeless person's advocate. Although it may look as though I have two roles, lecturer and minister, I experience them in a far more connected way than that.

Back to East Ham and Bonny Downs

In January 2015 we had accepted the call from Bonny Downs Baptist Church to return to a formal role as Senior Ministers. Dave had remained the Chair of Bonny Downs Community Association for all of the years we spent in the Docks and we felt the time was right to return to East Ham and steer the church and the community association back onto the same page. The decision was confirmed as we were struggling to think how to house Helen and her husband Donald with us and the Dos Santos family in Gatcombe Road. Physically we had just enough bed space, but we all knew it would be a squeeze. Out of the blue, a family at Bonny Downs, old friends from the very start of our journey, asked us if we would like to buy their parents' house at a reduced price. It stands directly opposite the old Bonny Downs church building and backs onto Flanders Field, where our community association runs so many sports and activities. Dave's parents helped us to buy it and we moved in in December 2017. You can hear the cricket and football from the garden and Dave has a shed where he can invite his Walking Football teammates back. We can even squeeze through our back fence to walk around Flanders field and the BDCA community garden and can keep an eye on the pavilion. I'm enjoying my first experience of having a study – or any kind of desk – and we are immensely grateful for this gift.

Church leadership 'beyond the billboard'

In this book, as in conversations with the *Journal of Missional Practice*, I have suggested that the 'billboard' of the institutional church is being well and truly shaken. Billboards are frames and structures telling us how to see something, making it intelligible, but also setting a boundary around it. Like all signs they carry messages and trap meanings. When I have suggested that the Western Church is like a billboard, I mean not only are its structures in a state of disrepair, with many denominations staring oblivion in the face, but the conceptual apparatus used to capture the message of Jesus is shaking loose. Doctrines which used to frame a 'Christian worldview' are increasingly challenged. Stuff is falling off the billboard. Doctrines which were once seen as beyond question are being interrogated. Some surmise that the Church is under attack and what is needed is a strident restatement of 'traditional views', on issues such as Biblical infallibility, Hell and sexuality. But I, like others, see that much of this revision is from honest Christians reflecting on their experiences and personal revelations, as well as those from other Christian traditions. Are Western Protestant churches, the stream of Christianity I am from, operating like dilapidated billboards? Has too much attention been given to attempts to 'fix the Church', rather than to look for what is beyond our man-made structures, and see a wilder, untamed vision beyond them?[27]

Falling church attendance, growing gaps in finance, and consumerist cultures undermine commitment to a local congregation. These are realities to face up to. Those who see this also predict that it will be far less possible for denominations to sustain full-time stipends for the traditional ministerial role of caretaking a congregation. The challenges of living as a minority culture in a multi-everything inner city, coupled with the cost of housing, may hasten the process in some places. So what is to be done? One path invites those called to lead churches to avoid challenging territory and to seek the remaining traditional posts in places where cultural Christianity still has purchase. Is that what Jesus modelled? The safe path? The broad way? The alternative is a journey beyond the billboard, beyond the practices and preoccupations of the institutional Church. Might there be a brighter, broader view ahead, that's been obscured by the structures of our institutions? Do ministers, in particular, spend far too much time attempting to 'fix the Church' that they have no time or energy to join with what God might be up to outside their institutions, out in the community, among so many 'Lydias'?

In a webinar with the Journal of Missional Practice, Al Roxburgh asked me what I felt ministers should do to be better prepared for ministry beyond the institutional Church. My off-the-cuff reply was 'read more, and not just the dead white men...stop going to church conferences... get a part-time job... spend less time in the church and more time meeting people in your community.'[28] This is my honest conclusion. These practices might not only make better ministers; they have the potential to make them better people

---

[27] *Journal of Missional Practice* http://journalofmissionalpractice.com/beyond-the-billboard-1-talk/

[28] This is from part 2 of a series of 3 conversations on 'life beyond the billboard'. See http://journalofmissionalpractice.com/billboard-2-leadership/

Of course, the implications here are not just for ministers, but are for all who follow Jesus. In Jesus' lifetime discipleship was not a programme of study, but an adventure in living out faith and then withdrawing to pray and think about what was learned, both together and in times of solitude. It was reflective praxis. Missional action in local communities was the starting place.

There is a Salvation Army hall here in Newham that has a placard over its door. It says, 'You are about to enter a place of worship'. It is written on the *inside* of its doorway. You read it just as you are about to step out into the street.

I love that.

Some questions to reflect on...
This chapter reflects that **shared living** and **bi-vocational** lives played a key part in the way God redefined how we see ourselves as 'ministers'. If the Western Church embraced these practices more widely, what do you imagine would happen?
Do you expereince your work/study/family life as an integral part of your faith, or in separate boxes? Are there consequences to how you approach this question?

7. BEING 'ROMAN BROTHERS AND SISTERS'

– a people of generous welcome

Acts 28:15 The brothers and sisters in Rome had heard we were coming, and they came to meet us at the Forum on the Appian Way. Others joined us at The Three Taverns. When Paul saw them, he was encouraged and thanked God.

In the last chapter of Acts Paul arrives on Italian shores, in virtual handcuffs, on his way to Rome. And what do the Roman 'brothers and sisters' do? They journey out to meet him and they take him to the pub. What a great welcome! 'The Three Taverns' is the equivalent of a modern-day service station on the way to Rome. It's a fair distance, about 50km. The name means, 'Three Shops'. It would have had a general store, a blacksmith's, and a refreshment house (OK, so not actually a pub, but you get my drift). When news reached them that Paul had finally landed on the coast, the Roman Church was not going to allow him to be taken into the city under arrest alone. They went out to meet him. Perhaps those who could pack quickly and travel immediately went ahead to get all the way down the Appian Way to the port at Ostia. The others would follow later to join up at The Three Taverns. Here's the thing, they all literally and metaphorically went out of their way to be a welcoming people.

When we preached on this passage at church, we flipped over to the list of names at the end of the Book of Romans in chapter 16 to find out who, most likely, made that journey to welcome Paul. There are **Priscilla and Aquila**, of course, lifelong friends, co-living co-workers; mature, educated, experienced, hospitable and committed. What a gift to the Roman Church they must have been! There are a surprising number of women named. One of them is **Mary,** who Paul said, 'worked very hard'. Women working hard in the church? Who'd have guessed! Paul uses the same phrase to describe the contribution of **Tryphena and Tryphosa.** We imagined them to be spinster sisters. There's a lovely irony in that their names mean 'dainty' and 'delicate' and yet they are called 'hard workers'. Their upmarket names suggest they were **aristocrats.** Before joining the Church they would not have worked for their livelihood, but there they are, getting their hands dirty in the 'hard work' of being church. Here come some of the church's recognised leaders. A couple, **Andronicus and Junia**, were perhaps part of the original Pentecost group filled with Spirit in Jerusalem. We know they had been active missionaries, and Paul describes them as 'fellow Jews who have been in prison with me.' He then famously says, 'they are outstanding among the apostles' (v. 7), a phrase which causes some scholars to turn intellectual pretzels as they twist to avoid the obvious inference that Junia, a woman, could have held such a designation. There are nobles sharing the resources of their 'large households', people like **Aristobulus** and **Narcissus.** For the first 300 years of the Christianity there wasn't a single church building, so people like the Roman nobles practiced radical hospitality and those blessed with spacious homes used them for gatherings. Here come some with Greek men's names: **Asyncritus, Phlegon, Hermes, Patrobas and Hermas.** We imagined them as group of young businessmen, living in bachelors' quarters. Here's another man coming along who possibly couldn't get out of work to make the whole trip so meets them at The Three Taverns. Look, he's being 'warmly greeted' by the businessmen! **Ampliatus,** such an interesting name. In the cemetery at Domitilla, archaeologists uncovered the early Christian catacombs of Rome and found a highly decorated tomb inscribed 'Ampliatus'. The use of only a first name usually suggested the man was born a slave. Yet this tomb was ornate, indicating the owner was highly respected, possibly a leader in the Roman Church.

In total there are 24 names in Paul's greetings to the Roman Church, 17 men and seven women. There are three house churches mentioned. The list suggests the extent to which social hierarchies were being dissolved in that community. Aristocratic women working? Slaves leading? Women spoken of as equal to their husbands? Could that really be what is hidden in the subtext? In something St Paul wrote?!

Can you imagine the other guests at The Three Taverns, the shock on their faces, as the 'brothers and sisters' gather? That weird group are eating together – but aren't they obviously Jews and Greeks of different classes? A similar thing happens when our church goes on a picnic. At our most recent Pentecost meal at Royal Docks Community Church we ate an Eritrean feast with people from eight different home languages – and there were only 30 or so of us. We dined with finance professionals and the kids the Dos Santos family scoop up from the streets on the way to our gatherings. There's no earthly reason why such a diverse crowd should be such close friends. It's a Kingdom feast.

The tightrope-walk of community

So, the book of Acts closes with one more important encounter for Paul, and this time it's not an individual, but a collective. It's the Church as it should be: a diverse, welcoming, city of refuge. Rome will be where Paul spends years under house arrest, but he won't be alone: the Roman 'brothers and sisters' are with him. The early Church in Rome was an amazing example of a place where encounters with 'Others' were possible. It can't have been plain sailing to be part of it: surrounded by a transient population; political and religious powers against them; the stretch of diversity; the issues of class and ethnicity. This sounds familiar. Our reflection on ministry in East London is that there is a wealth of treasure found in a diverse church family. Angie once preached about church community. She challenged us to think beyond seeing the church as a safety net, something we hope will be there if we need it. Although, please God the church community always will be a place that people who 'fall from grace' fall into, Angie went further. It's not just the net; the church community is the tightrope itself. It's the scary, risky, wobbly walk we make together. Are you up for this tightrope walk? Are you mature enough to be part of a diverse, welcoming, community church?

Returning to Bonny Downs, to live in the area and minister again in our former congregation, set us on our own tightrope walk. It began with a wobble. Having become accustomed to the culture of inclusion and the freer forms of community life in the Docks church, it was a bit of a shock to be in a place which had more formality and 'churchiness'. It wasn't the Bonny Downs we remembered. But this church was our first love and the call to return was very clear.

The tightrope well and truly quivered when the issue of LGTB+ inclusion came up. Like other congregations, Bonny Downs faced the challenge putting into words some of the things that had been unsaid. Were lesbian and gay people and those of different gender identities truly welcome as equals in our church? Could we really have one congregation which was fully inclusive and another which held the policy of 'don't ask, don't tell?' But we too had heard words like Peter heard in his God-dream: 'don't call unclean what I call clean'. Like Peter with Cornelius, the Gentiles were at the door. There were lesbian and gay people in the church at Bonny Downs and several families had spoken to me about their children coming out. Were they welcome? What did we think? I gave a theology seminar which I hoped would restore my own integrity – laying out 'here's what I believe, others will differ, but let's do so with charity'. In the coming weeks around ten people left the church. You might think, that doesn't sound too painful; those numbers can be absorbed. But that's not how it feels when people you are a minister to leave your community. We offered to meet, we sought to explain this issue was not a fundamental and reassure them that conversations would continue so that we could journey together, but they left anyway. Today I'm relieved we had this wobble early on the journey. We cannot be a part of, let alone lead, a church that has an 'Us and Them' mentality on this issue. I don't think it should ever have become such a divisive matter within the Church more generally. I took some comfort in the fact that there were plenty of alternative local congregations for those who had left that would share their views and priorities. What is more, those who stayed, and the increasing number of wonderful LGBT+ people in both congregations, would be truly welcome, and there just aren't many Evangelical churches where that is genuinely the case.

Communion on a park bench

Other stories of being a truly inclusive, welcoming church are more fun to recount. Like the time I gave a dog communion on a park bench. It was during the prayer walk to mark the beginning of a new circuit of the NewWay Winter Night Shelter. Angie, Matthew and Jonny led the group on a nine mile walk around the host churches, praying against issues of injustice and crying out to God for mercy. The walk ended with a meal at Bonny Downs, cooked by a group of Hindu and Muslim women who learn English in the old mission building. Before the meal, we shared communion in Central Park, East Ham. Around six homeless people joined us, including three who had been living in a tent in the park. We know these people well. They are regulars at the Wednesday Community Meal, and Angie and Jonny had been advocating for them for years, all without much success. Winter was coming. We could offer places in the night shelter, except for one problem: no dogs allowed. Rocky Rambler the 'Staffie' would hear the proverbial Christmas message, 'No Room!'

Communion on a park bench is wonderful.[29] We shared what it meant to know that Jesus had been broken too. His brokenness and spilled-out life could become 're-membered' within us in this special meal. I bought hot Afghan bread especially for the sacrament, and lots of it, because the prayer walkers and park sleepers would most likely be hungry. But Rocky got scent of the hot bread and he would not be deterred. Either I was going to have to attempt to lead communion from under a Staffie or I was going to have to feed him surreptitious scraps of bread while I said the words and prayed the prayers. So Rocky got to take communion, much to his owner's delight. My mum was there, gently chuckling and sitting down on the makeshift altar of the bench to chat and pray with one of the homeless men. 'Oi Ellen!' he said, 'You are sitting on the body of Christ!' She was! A spare loaf of bread was still on the bench. We didn't rush away from this holy gathering; we stayed and prayed for people individually, including our three friends with their tent in the park and then we invited everyone back for the Indian meal at the church. This was a lovely snapshot of the Kingdom of God - the old Bonny Downs kitchen full of hijab-wearing neighbours cooking food for the prayer-walkers and homeless guests. And can you guess? I almost don't want to say it as I hate endings that are too tidy. All three of our park friends were rehoused into residential rehab and accommodation that winter. And through the wonders of WhatsApp, Rocky

---

[29] See picture on the 'Looking for Lydia' tab on www.bonnydownschurch.org

himself was offered a foster home in leafy Essex with a huge garden and doggie friends to play with. He's still there! I don't know what to think about giving communion to dogs. I don't know what I think about a lot of things I find myself doing as a minister in East Ham. But I know what I feel. I feel love and grace in the crazy stuff. I find laughter and fun among the people I walk the tightrope of community with. And please don't think I'm saying that we can just start a series of little communion services on park benches and imagine it will end homelessness. It is the hard work of running night shelters, and providing skilled advocacy, along with the resilience of years of prayer which achieves transformation. But, I think, sometimes the Spirit of God wants to have fun and sends errant Staffies along to keep us on our toes.

Sermon cooking

'Inclusion' is becoming the word running through the rock of church life in both of our congregations. Those years of church around tables, sharing Bible stories with people who had never heard them before, have shaped the way I handle the Bible and the way I go about the task of preparing sermons. As I took responsibility for planning the teaching series and leading preaching teams in both congregations, I introduced our own particular method of sermon preparation. Everyone who wants to preach regularly must prepare their sermon in at least one community conversation. For unknown reasons we call this 'cooking a sermon'. I cook mine in the Foodbank, with women's gatherings or youth groups and by chatting to homeless people in the park. I natter my way through the story and fill clipboards and notebooks with scribblings. Others use toddler groups, conversations with football teams, Sunday school classes and coffee with friends. The aim is to include at least some people who will never have heard the Bible passage before and are very unlikely to listen to a church sermon. Ideally it's a process that takes a good few weeks of listening before a few hours of writing and less than 30 minutes of preaching. To achieve this, we have long sermon series and give our preachers lots of advance notice of the passage they have to 'cook'. It's a simple and flexible technique. So how might you cook a sermon? Tell a group of people that you have to preach soon and tell them the outline of the story (sometimes I stop midway and get people to guess what comes next) then be humble, gather questions, comments, observations and answers to particular questions. The insights, anecdotes and wisdom from the streets are fresh manna for our Sunday reflections. It's a counter-hierarchical way to gather knowledge. And it's much more fun than sitting in an office with a concordance. Of course, preachers need a level of theological knowledge and the gift of communication, but God's promise is to speak to all people. The Bible says that; do we ministers believe it? The gift of teaching is part and parcel of the tightrope-walk of being church in our community, not just on Sundays. Crafting knowledge together is not always comfortable. Sometimes it feels that we ask more questions than we answer. Our method of preparing sermons takes the diversity of our community seriously and it sometimes expresses the messy nature of how we experience life and God. Some of the stories we use to illustrate points in our preaching are problematic, but they are our experiences, and they speak of the presence of God with us, in our particular place. Contextualising theology is more precarious than giving pat answers, and the wisdom we gather feels provisional. We are learning together how to put into words ideas about God. Sometimes these conversations lead to new liturgy, prayers and poems, written for the Sunday congregation to include in worship. We are working on ways to compile this contextual liturgy, but it's tricky because how do you capture such a living, moving thing? Time to discuss and reflect with people who are part of the midweek ministries that form the 'blurry-edge' of the church gives us a great two-way street for Word and worship. Meeting so many people who say, 'I don't know the right answer, but ...' frees me to admit the same.

Ash Wednesday in the Foodbank

Sometimes, even the most 'Low Church' of us, even Baptists, feel the need for a bit of ritual. Last year, instead of cooking my sermon in the Foodbank, I set up an Ash Wednesday table there and told the people that I was there to 'burn regrets'. Armed with tissue paper and oil to mix ashes, and a prayer that I would not set the fire alarms off, I waited for guests to be intrigued enough to come over. I had a steady stream of people suggesting words which captured their regrets and failings. We wrote them on the tissue and burnt them on a plate. Then I poured oil over them, explaining 'God's love and forgiveness are bigger than our sins and regrets'. I started drawing crosses with the ashes onto people's foreheads. Until Mohammed came to the table. Cultural minefields lay across the path ahead, so I changed tack. 'Mohammed, what do Muslims pray to ask God for forgiveness?' Mohammed shared a beautiful prayer in Arabic and I asked him to translate it into English so our church could use those words on Sunday. 'But you haven't burnt my words', he said. So we did. We wrote down the words that captured this man's sense of loss and isolation and set them alight. Now what to do with the ashes? The smudgy crosses on people's foreheads were drawing attention. 'Shall I put a smudge on your hand, Mohammed?' 'No. Put a cross on my forehead.' Who can argue with that? A few weeks later we were getting our kitchen refitted in the new East Ham house. It was the usual East End way of approaching building works – you ask anyone who knows how to do something, and others who might owe you a favour, to help. And there was Mohammed, invited by my brother-in-law to help with the electrical work. He was perched on a ladder fitting spotlights into the ceiling. I didn't know we were having spotlights. I didn't know we were asking Mohammed. 'Sally, the burning words worked,' he said. It took me a moment, but I realised he was speaking about Ash Wednesday. 'Look at me! Fixing the minister's kitchen! The burning words are working!' And they were. They do.

An inn on the way

We hope this book has given some insight into the journey we have taken in 'Looking for Lydia'. What sort of community church can I now see growing from this 20-year journey? Jayne Ozanne, a well-known Anglican and member of the Church of England's General Synod, gave a sermon which inspired the way I want to describe what I see.[30]

The followers of Jesus are called to build communities which serve as 'an inn on the way' – a meeting place for people on a journey. The Christian community I see is a place to share stories, compare conceptual maps, warn of dangers and enjoy a good meal. Inns are open to everyone and judged by the quality of their welcome. You can have a good time in an inn. All life is there. It's a place on the way to a better destination. The church is like that. One thing the church is not is a fortress. That would be a place to retreat to and shut out the world; where only 'insiders' are welcome and everyone else is seen as a threat. It would be a place to receive instructions but not ask questions. There are guards on the gates, barricades and moats; all manner of barriers to keep the insiders in and the outsiders out. Neither do I see Christian communities as cosy cottages. In the early years of the Anglican movement Richard Hooker reputedly

---

[30] Jane Ozanne's sermon can be read here http://www.jayneozanne.com/

prayed, 'I pray that none will be offended if I seek to make the Christian religion an inn where all are received joyously, rather than a cottage where some few friends of the family are to be received.' This sounds like a wonderful way to imagine churches. It sounds like a God-dream worth working for.

Looking for Lydia?

As we reflect on our story, we hope that those who wish to journey out from church as we have known it, and 'look for Lydia' will hear a call to live with generous hospitality among those at the margins; a counter-cultural, downwardly-mobile life which intrigues and challenges. It is to live with an openness to encounter strangers and outsiders, and be surprised to find that we didn't bring God to these places and people: God is already there. It will take 'remainers, returners and relocators'[31]- people who choose to stay in, return or relocate to marginalised communities – to enflesh hope in those neighbourhoods. And it's not enough just to say we *hope* for God to transform these places from a distance. I believe we need to be there, among those feeling hopeless. Faith is not really expressed through signing up to a list of doctrinal statements, but through *how* we live; the choices we make about *where* we live and *who* we live among. I'm with Ched Myers, 'Hope is where your arse is!'[32]

---

[31] This description of three types of people is originally by John Perkins. I encountered these ideas listening to Ash Barker. See Ash's book *Slum Life Rising* (UNOH Publishing, 2012) to learn how these principles worked out in Klong Thoey, Thailand, a community Ash and Anji Barker lived and worked in for 12 years

[32] We heard Ched Myers give a talk with this title at Greenbelt in 2007. It's available here: https://www.greenbelt.org.uk/talks/hope-is-where-your-arse-is/

Pause for thought...
*This chapter has tried to shine a spotlight on the need for churches to see themselves as welcoming '**inns on the way**'. What do you make of the metaphor?*

*How important is the practice of **intentional inclusion** in your faith community?*

*We described a method of preparing church teaching, which we call '**cooking the sermon**', and the theory of knowledge behind it. How might teaching and learning be organised to help people hear God together? How might your community go further into this?*

*'**Remainers, returners and relocators'** all share one thing in common – they see where they live as an intentional part of being a disciple of Jesus. Have you thought about this for yourself? Why do you live where you do?*

CONTACTS & USEFUL LINKS

Bonny Downs Baptist Church
www.bonnydownschurch.org
(Incl. 'Looking for Lydia' tab with photos to accompany this book)

Royal Docks Community Church
www.royaldockschurche16.com

Bonny Downs Community Association
www.bonnydowns.org

NewWay winter night shelter
https://www.newwayproject.org/

Journal of Missional Practice
www.journalofmissionalpractice.com

Red Letter Christians
www.redletterchristians.org
in the UK: https://redletterchristians.uk
www.facebook.com/redletterchristiansuk

Our young leaders benefitted greatly from training in urban ministry with
https://urbanchangemakers.org/

25107801R00047

Printed in Great Britain
by Amazon